The
SOLO SENIOR'S
GUIDE TO THRIVE

Planning for Legal, Financial, and Personal Well-Being

Includes Solo Senior Organizer Workbook

KATHY L. McNAIR ESQ.
Elder Law Attorney

The Solo Senior's Guide to Thrive:
Planning for Legal, Financial, and Personal Well-Being

Published by Solo Allies
www.SoloAllies.com

ISBN (Paperback): 979-8-9987754-0-6
ISBN (eBook): 979-8-9987754-1-3

Printed in the United States of America
First Edition

Cover design by Sinisa Poznanovic
Interior design and layout by AtalantaCreative.ca

Disclaimer: The information provided in this book is for general educational and informational purposes only and is not a substitute for legal, medical, or financial advice. Consult with a qualified professional regarding your specific situation.

ACKNOWLEDGEMENTS

This book would not have been possible without the support, insight, and encouragement of many incredible people and organizations. First, I would like to thank my husband, David McNair. Your support at home and work made it possible for me to carve out the time and focus needed to write this book.

Thank you to my editor, Irena Joannides, whose thoughtful guidance and careful edits helped shape this book, and to Sinisa Poznanovic, for designing the book cover.

Thank you to my editor, Irena Joannides, whose thoughtful guidance and careful edits helped shape this book, and to Sinisa Poznanovic, for designing the book cover.

To the following Elder Law attorneys across the country, thank you for your contributions to the field and for your support of seniors:

- **Shana Siegel** with Norris McLaughlin Attorneys at Law in New Jersey, NY, and host of the *Aging Answers Podcast.*

- **Harry Margolis,** whose Elder Law course at Boston College Law School helped me discover my passion. He is a nationally recognized Elder Law Attorney with Margolis & Bloom and the author of *Get Your Ducks in a Row.*

- **H. Frances Reeves**, founder of Parent Your Parents, and author of *Boomers Booming: How to Thrive after Sixty-Five,* who provides invaluable services to Solo Seniors in Florida.

- **Abigail Wolf Stanton,** serving the Metro Washington, D.C. area, Virginia and Maryland, with The Elder and Disability Law Center.

- **Lisa Powers** in the Rochester and Ithaca area, New York, with Harris Beach Murtha, Attorneys at Law.

I am also grateful to the following thought leaders on solo aging:

- **Vanya Drumchiyska** of *Sixty and Me* for her powerful message of positive aging and the vibrant community she has built.
- **Sara Zeff Geber,** thought leader, speaker, and author of *Essential Retirement Planning for Solo Agers*, whose pioneering work continues to shape the conversation about aging alone.
- **Carol Marak,** author and solo aging advocate.
- **Eric Blake**, Certified Financial Planner and host of *The Simply Retirement Podcast*, in McKinney, Texas.

To the community groups and organizations that continue to support and inspire this work:

- **The Kinship for the Kinless Group**
- **The Winchester Solo Ager Network**
- **The Massachusetts Chapter of the National Academy of Elder Law Attorneys**—thank you for your ongoing community, support, and advocacy to help seniors in Massachusetts thrive.

And finally, to my team at Senior Solutions Attorneys at Law LLC:

- **Amy Mullen,** a dedicated and compassionate attorney with a deep commitment to helping seniors.
- **David McNair,** my husband, and a fantastic attorney, whose support makes everything possible.
- **Kelly Morton, Rachel Mannion, and Judy Mata**—thank you for your dedication, organization, and the many behind-the-scenes efforts to keep our office running smoothly.

I also want to thank the many solo seniors who have welcomed me into their groups, shared their concerns, and helped envision a more supported future.

CONTENTS

PART II: PLANNING FOR A SECURE FINANCIAL FUTURE

PART III: HOUSING, COMMUNITY, AND END-OF-LIFE CARE

PART IV: SOLO SENIOR ORGANIZER

INTRODUCTION

Why I Wrote This Book

In my 25 years of practicing Elder Law and Estate Planning, I have had the privilege of working with many solo seniors—individuals aging without family support. My role often extends beyond legal planning.

In some cases, judges appointed me to make decisions for solo seniors who never planned and could no longer care for themselves. In other cases, my clients planned for their future and knew they did not have someone they could count on to help if needed. They chose me to make critical decisions if they could no longer do so. Each case has taught me so much about the unique needs of solo seniors and the importance of thoughtful and proactive planning.

I wrote this book to encourage and empower solo seniors to take control of their future. Planning ahead and building connections can ensure your wishes are honored if you need support. Simply having legal documents is not enough—you also need to identify the people who will stand by you in a crisis.

Planning + People = Peace of Mind ™

This simple formula forms the foundation of thriving as a solo senior.

I have met many solo seniors who failed to plan and lost control over their lives. They were often smart people. Why didn't they plan? They will never have a chance to tell their story. I was part of their lives, acting as their decision-maker until they died. With this unique perspective, I wrote this book, hoping that it would serve as a useful guide to empower solo seniors to be proactive about planning for their future.

Who Is This Book For?

This book is for anyone who does not have close family to rely upon as they age. Some may be single, divorced, or widowed. Others may be married but don't have children. When one spouse dies or gets sick, the other will be a solo senior unless they have a strong support network.

Sometimes, solo seniors have adult children they care for very much but who cannot assist them as they age. Perhaps they have a developmentally delayed or mentally ill child. Others have adult children who cannot be depended upon or who may be struggling with addiction or gambling. Sometimes, children live far away, have busy lives, and cannot care for their parents. Other solo seniors are independent and may not want their family involved or simply prefer to have a neutral person make those decisions if the time comes. There are no guarantees in life, and even those with family may find themselves without the support they need.

Considering the number of people aging without the support of family, the term "solo senior" describes at least 25% of adults over the age of 55 in the United States, and this number is growing.

What This Book Will Help You Do

- Understand the critical decisions you need to make as a solo senior
- Identify and connect with the right people who can support you
- Get organized and create a holistic plan for your future
- Feel empowered to live your best life as you age

I hope this book will inspire you to take charge of your future, find the support you need, and thrive.

Kathy McNair

PART I:
LEGAL PLANNING
FOR SOLO SENIORS

1. THE CONSEQUENCES OF FAILING TO PLAN

"The trouble is you think you have time." — *Buddha*

Aging alone can be challenging. While we know we must plan for our future, procrastinating is easy. We might think we have plenty of time, feel unsure about where to start or find the idea of aging depressing. None of us can predict what life will bring, but there is one crucial step we can take: preparing as best we can. Planning can make the difference between successfully navigating aging and feeling out of control.

This chapter will discuss the legal and practical consequences of failing to plan. As a Guardian and Conservator, I have worked closely with solo seniors who never planned. My involvement was brief in some cases, while it lasted as long as 25 years in others. These experiences have given me a unique perspective on planning for the future.

I will start by sharing two real-life examples with you. By understanding the problems that may arise, I hope you will be motivated to take proactive steps to protect your autonomy, dignity, and wishes, whatever the future may bring.

Please note that all names in these stories are changed to ensure privacy.

Tom

Tom was a brilliant man in his late 70s. An Ivy League graduate, he retired from a successful career and worked part-time at a library to stay busy. One day, he fell on the ice and hit his head. He was rushed to the hospital. When the hospital sent him home, he was so overwhelmed by being alone that he sat on the steps of his apartment building, crying for hours and asking for help. Eventually, a neighbor called the police, and they took Tom back to the hospital.

He was admitted to the Geriatric Psychiatric Unit, where a doctor decided that he could not make medical or financial decisions for himself due to mild dementia. Since he did not have a Health Care Proxy or a Power of Attorney, the hospital attorney went to court to seek the appointment of a Guardian to make medical and personal decisions for him and a Conservator to manage his finances. Tom received a legal notice informing him about this and providing instructions to follow if he disagreed.

Tom waited in the hospital for almost two months until the court appointed me as his Guardian and Conservator. He seemed relieved to see me. My priority was getting him out of the hospital and keeping him safe and less isolated.

Tom did not want to return to his apartment. I had to find out what kind of care and housing he could afford. I contacted his landlord and obtained a key to his apartment. My assistant and I looked for any information that might give us some clue about his bank accounts or financial assets. We also gathered his clothes as, for the past two months, he wore a hospital gown or clothes donated to the hospital. Tom probably never thought two strangers would enter his apartment to search for these things or that he would not return home.

I helped Tom move into an assisted living facility, where he had his own studio apartment. I bought furniture and art for his walls, guessing what he would have chosen, and brought a few photos of his parents. Overall, Tom was happy to be part of a community. He especially liked that there were three meals each day and nurses and aides to help him. Tom was there for a few years until he started to run low on funds. I had to move him to another assisted living facility that would accept Medicaid benefits. That move was hard on him. Had Tom planned, he *would have had time to wait for an affordable option, avoiding two moves. Shortly after the move, Tom had a stroke. His condition worsened significantly, and I returned to court to obtain an order to allow him to receive hospice care instead of aggressive medical care to prolong his life artificially.*

As Tom's Conservator, I was obligated to file financial reports, including providing the court with a list of his financial assets and an account of how I spent his money. After receiving the court's approval, I paid myself from Tom's funds. Tom's financial information became a public record. Most people would not want their private financial information available for anyone to see.

Tom's story highlights how even an incredibly smart and capable person can face a difficult situation and lose control over their life without sufficient planning. Tom appreciated having a Guardian and Conservator. However, some people, like Sophie, have a very different reaction, often a profound sense of loss.

Sophie

Sophie, a 96-year-old woman originally from Scotland, was very feisty. She didn't have any family or close friends. She was a nanny when she was younger, but she was retired for some time and lived alone.

The court appointed me as her Guardian and Conservator when she was hospitalized for dehydration and an inability to care for herself due to dementia. Sophie was mad about losing her rights. She asked about the judge who appointed me and held up her fist, yelling his name like she would let him have it. When I went to Sophie's home, her windows were broken, the lightbulbs burned out, and she had no heat. Her electricity was turned off because she hadn't paid the bill. She owned a two-family home, and the tenants had not paid rent in a long time. It wasn't safe for her to return home, and she could not care for herself.

I hired a senior living consultant to take Sophie on a tour of several assisted living facilities so that she could choose the one she liked best. During the tour, she tricked him into driving by her home, where she rolled down the windows and screamed, "I've been kidnapped; help me!" Poor Sophie was distraught about losing her independence. She was a very religious woman, and she moved into a Catholic facility, where they held Mass each day. I arranged for a private companion to visit her frequently and take her for lunch or walks. After a few years, she adjusted and was content. When she died, the nursing home held a memorial service. Besides a few residents and the nuns, no one came except her companion and me.

Sophie's story highlights how difficult losing your autonomy can be. Had she planned, she could have picked the person who would help her and feel more in control over her life.

Guardianship and Conservatorship

Tom and Sophie's stories illustrate what could happen if you become incapable of making decisions for yourself and managing your affairs. When you do not have the proper legal documents in place, or the people named in those documents are not available to help you, the court will appoint a Guardian and Conservator. Let's get a better understanding of these two roles by starting with the definitions:

A Legal Guardian is someone appointed by a court or with the legal authority and duty to make decisions about the well-being and medical care of a person deemed incompetent.

A Conservator handles the financial affairs of a person deemed incompetent by a court.

Appointing a Guardian and Conservator can take months. You may wait in the hospital during this time. In your darkest hour, a stranger could introduce themselves to you as your Guardian and Conservator. You will have lost your rights to make decisions about where you will live, what medical care you will receive, and even who can visit you.

Guardians and Conservators often have limited information about those they are entrusted to make decisions for. Usually, the only information they have is in their medical records. They will try their best to piece together information about you, including what assets you own, what insurance you have, and whether you have any family or friends. It is like a scavenger hunt: finding clues in your mail, asking the IRS for your tax records, looking through your home, and talking to anyone involved who knows you.

A stranger will decide how your money is spent, whether you will ever return to your home, and what happens to your personal belongings. It may take months to get your clothes and belongings. They will buy new clothes for you, guessing your size and style, but probably getting it wrong. You will lose your independence and autonomy as an adult.

I am not trying to scare you, but I want to emphasize how important planning is in protecting your wishes and dignity as you age. There is a better way to spend your final years than being subjected to Guardianship or Conservatorship.

Most Guardians are honest, kind, and caring people who want to help others. However, they are still strangers in charge of another person's future, finances, and life. As someone who has served as Guardian and Conservator, I know how difficult it is to guess what the person's wishes are when I meet them for the first time in the hospital when they are sick, scared, and suffering from cognitive impairment.

It is easier to help someone if I meet them before a crisis when they have a clear mind and time to plan. I can get to know them, understand what is important to them, obtain their instructions, and honor their wishes.

A fictional movie on Netflix called "I Care a Lot" depicts an evil Guardian who exploits older people. The story involves a corrupt lawyer, doctor, and nursing home director who work together to take advantage of a competent woman. If you are a senior living alone and have seen this film, it may scare you into taking steps to safeguard yourself. While some people target and exploit seniors, especially those living alone, this movie is very unrealistic. When you have a solid estate plan, including proper legal documents, and you have people named in those documents who you can rely upon to be there for you when needed, there is no need to worry about being placed under Guardianship and Conservatorship.

Here are some common questions about Guardianship and Conservatorship. This information is based on Massachusetts law, but most states have a similar process.

Common Questions About Guardianship and Conservatorship

Who can ask that a Guardian and Conservator be appointed?

Hospitals, Social Service Agencies, and Adult Protective Services often file Guardianship or Conservatorship court petitions for those who can no longer make their own decisions. When the person has no one willing or able to serve in this role, the court will appoint an attorney like myself.

If a relative, friend, neighbor, or anyone concerned about you believes you cannot care for yourself, they can also request Guardianship and Conservatorship. They can ask to appoint themselves or another person in these roles.

How is incapacity determined?

Before anyone can ask the court to appoint a Guardian or Conservator, they must obtain medical evidence explaining why you cannot care for yourself. A medical doctor must meet with you to make this determination and prepare paperwork to submit to the court as evidence. The most typical reasons for granting Guardianship and Conservatorship are dementia, Alzheimer's, aphasia, stroke, or accidents that make it challenging to communicate.

How is the Guardian and Conservator's suitability determined?

The court will appoint a suitable person, usually giving preference to a family member who is willing and able to take the job. Judges determine suitability in different ways, such as running a criminal record background check, appointing a professional with Guardianship experience, or choosing a family member capable of handling the responsibilities. As mentioned, when a family member or friend is unavailable, the court usually appoints an attorney.

Can I object to Guardianship and Conservatorship?

When someone files a petition for Guardianship and Conservatorship with the court, you must receive a written notice informing you about it. You will have a certain amount of time to object. If you object, you can hire an attorney or ask the court to appoint an attorney to represent you.

If you have any known close relatives, the person who filed the petition must also notify them. They, too, can object if they do not think the proposed Guardian and Conservator is the best choice. If you do not have any known relatives, the person filing the petition must publish a notice in the newspaper. It will notify any possible family members that a petition for Guardianship and Conservatorship has been filed and include instructions on how to object. This notice is published only in one newspaper, one time, and typically in a local publication. In one of my cases, a woman's first cousin saw it and contacted me. Otherwise, I would not have known about her. Most people probably don't read the legal notice section of the newspaper and are unlikely to see this.

If you or a family member files an objection with the court, there will likely be a trial. Usually, you will wait in the hospital during this time. If you demand to leave but cannot care for yourself, a judge could force you to stay.

How much control does the Guardian have over my life?

The Guardian will have total control over your life unless limited by the court. They will decide where you should live, whether you should go to a nursing home, what medical care you should receive, what happens to your possessions, who can visit you, whether you can travel or go out for lunch or activities. When a Guardian is appointed, you lose your freedom to decide for yourself as an adult. You can no longer legally sign documents like consent forms or contracts. The Guardian makes all decisions for you, like a parent does for a child under 18.

How much control does the Conservator have over my assets?

If a Conservator is appointed, they can access your financial accounts, open and close bank accounts, and invest and spend your money for your benefit. They may also buy or sell real estate for you with additional permission from the court.

Are Guardians and Conservators monitored?

The court often requires the Guardian or Conservator to file reports about your well-being or finances. There is significant variation in how courts monitor Guardians, how frequently they review the case, and what happens if reports are late or missing. However, the court may remove a Guardian or Conservator who does not comply with the reporting requirements.

Sometimes, judges appoint a Guardian ad Litem to ensure that the Guardian or Conservator acts in your best interest. Usually, a Guardian ad Litem is an attorney. They will examine the financial activity and prepare a report to assist the judge. The person under Conservatorship and their family must also receive notice when reports are filed so they can review them.

Who pays the Guardian and Conservator?

Unless you are broke, everyone appointed by the court to represent you or involved in the case will get paid with your money. This includes attorneys, the Guardian ad Litem, and your Guardian or Conservator. The Guardian and Conservator will continue to bill you for as long as they serve in this role. The costs and legal fees are much more expensive than planning and being prepared. I have seen fees as high as $650 per hour and costs, expenses, and fees of $100,000 per year or more.

What happens if a Conservator mishandles my assets or steals from me?

In most cases, the court will require that the person appointed as Conservator file a bond with sureties. A bond is a signed statement stating they will not mishandle or steal assets. In most cases, it is backed by sureties. Insurance companies provide sureties, similar to an insurance policy, to guarantee that they will cover the loss if the Conservator steals or mishandles the funds.

I knew a respected attorney who served as Conservator for many people. He hired a financial advisor to invest the money for the people he was appointed to protect. The investments were high-risk and caused substantial losses for the people he was supposed to protect. The attorney was suspended from practicing law, and the surety company had to pay for the losses. The Conservator never should have invested in such a high-risk way.

Can a Guardianship and Conservatorship be terminated?

Unless the appointment is temporary, the Guardianship or Conservatorship does not end unless the court terminates it or upon death. The court can terminate a Guardianship or Conservatorship if circumstances change and medical evidence supports this.

How can I protect myself from the court appointing a Guardian or Conservator for me?

You can protect yourself by planning while you are still mentally competent by signing legal documents to appoint someone you trust to act on your behalf if you cannot do so yourself. Specifically, you should complete a Health Care Proxy for medical decisions and a Durable Power of Attorney for financial matters. The next chapter will discuss these critical roles and documents in greater detail.

Many people assume that if they have a spouse or family members, they can automatically step in and make decisions without legal documents. Unfortunately, this is not the case. Without a valid Health Care Proxy and Durable Power of Attorney, even your closest family must go to court to ask to be appointed as your Guardian and/or Conservator. This process can be stressful, expensive, and uncertain.

• • • •

Most people hope they will remain independent and die in their sleep without any decline in their ability to take care of themselves. Realistically, most of us will need some help as we get older. The assistance may only be needed briefly, but we have no way of knowing. Planning for whatever situation may arise is the best way to protect yourself and avoid losing control.

2. THE HEALTH CARE PROXY

"A good plan today is better than a perfect plan tomorrow."
— *George S. Patton*

As we saw in the previous chapter, not planning could mean losing control over your medical care, life, and finances. If you have a health emergency or can no longer understand what is happening, a court-appointed Guardian and Conservator, potentially a stranger, could make critical decisions on your behalf.

At a minimum, every adult—whether they are aging alone or surrounded by a supportive family—should have three key legal documents in place to protect themselves:

> 1. *A Health Care Proxy*
> 2. *A Durable Power of Attorney*
> 3. *A Last Will and Testament*

The first two documents ensure that someone you trust will manage your medical care and your legal and financial affairs in case of an emergency or incapacity. The third ensures your wishes will be honored after your death.

This chapter will focus on the Health Care Proxy. We will start with an example of good planning, with the story of one of my favorite clients, Margaret:

Margaret

Margaret came from a close-knit Italian family and lived with two of her sisters in a two-family house. Their husbands had died, and they did not have children. Margaret and her sisters met with me while they were still independent and in their 70s.

Each sister implemented an estate plan, intending to take care of each other.

Margaret helped her sisters, Rose and Ruth, as they needed more care. Eventually, they each needed expensive nursing home care. I helped Margaret apply for Medicaid benefits for her sisters so they could get the care they needed. I protected their home, which was worth a considerable amount for Margaret.

After caring for her sisters, Margaret recognized that no one would be there to care for her if she needed help. She asked me to act as her Health Care Proxy, Power of Attorney, and Personal Representative (or Executor) of her estate.

After her sisters died, Margaret remained at home. When she needed more help, I hired caregivers for her. She was not interested in moving to an assisted living facility. She had a few friends who cared deeply about her. They went to church and bingo together each week. Eventually, Margaret was diagnosed with dementia, and it became difficult to live at home safely without significantly more care.

When Margaret's furnace broke in the middle of winter, she had to go somewhere during the repair. I arranged for her to spend two weeks at a respite program at a nearby assisted living facility. She had a wonderful time there and was surprised by how much she enjoyed the social interactions and community, so she decided to stay. She had her own apartment, which we decorated with some new items and some cherished items from her home, like a beautiful photograph of her from her younger days and pictures of her husband, parents, and sisters.

Margaret had a wonderful lifelong friend who visited several times per week. I also hired private caregivers to spend time with her. Margaret had saved the daily letters her husband had sent to her when he was away in the military. As she declined, her companion would read these beautiful love letters to her.

She was well taken care of and supported at the end of her life.

Her close friends, the nuns, and I attended her funeral just as she had wanted. She was buried with her sisters, and her remaining funds were distributed to the nuns, according to her Will. By planning in advance, Margaret's wishes were honored, and she lived her life well until the end.

The Health Care Proxy Legal Document

A Health Care Proxy (also called a "Power of Attorney for Health Care" or a "Health Care Surrogate") is a legal document that allows you to designate someone to make medical decisions for you when you can no longer make them yourself. It only goes into effect once a doctor decides you cannot communicate your wishes or understand.

If you have ever been admitted to a hospital, you may have signed a Health Care Proxy there. This document lets the hospital know who will make medical decisions if you cannot communicate or understand while in their care. However, the hospital form is usually generic and not enough for solo seniors. Even if you have signed a Health Care Proxy during a hospital stay, you should have a Health Care Proxy document drafted by an attorney to ensure that you will be protected.

Choosing a Person to Act as Your Health Care Proxy

When naming a Health Care Proxy, choose someone who will honor your wishes. Before you name someone, you should ensure the person is willing to take the job. You cannot force anyone to act as your Health Care Proxy, even if you choose them.

Most solo seniors have friends of the same age. These friends may be suitable, but it is important to name a backup Health Care Proxy.

Tips for Choosing a Friend or Family Member as Your Health Care Proxy

Selecting the right person to serve as your Health Care Proxy is one of the most important decisions you will make. Here are a few key factors to consider when choosing someone for this role:

- **Ask Them First:** Before naming someone as your Health Care Proxy, have an honest conversation to ensure they are willing and able to take on this responsibility. If you surprise someone with this, they may not be willing or available to help you when needed.

- **Reliability Is Essential:** Your Health Care Proxy should be someone you can count on to act responsibly and follow your wishes.

- **Age and Availability:** Ideally, choose someone younger than you who lives locally or is willing to travel at short notice. Emergencies can happen anytime, and having a proxy who can show up when needed is critical.

- **Have Backups:** If possible, name multiple backups in case your primary choice is unavailable. It is vital for solo seniors, whose friends or family may be the same age as you.

Get Creative: Building Relationships for Support

Finding someone to serve as your Health Care Proxy can be difficult if you don't have family to rely on. The key is to start building relationships and try to be a person who is there to support others—you never know where a strong connection might form. Start with small acts of kindness and connection. Here are some ideas:

- If you have neighbors, offer to lend a hand—watch the kids for an hour, invite them over, or show you care.

- As you know someone better, asking if someone would be willing to serve as your Health Care Proxy becomes easier. Many people are glad to help but may not realize you need someone to take on this role.

- Connect with other solo seniors.

- Most towns have a Senior Center, which can be a great starting place to meet others in similar situations. Consider forming a small group with other solo seniors looking for mutual support. A group of three to six solo seniors could agree to serve as Health Care Proxies for each other. While only one person can act at a time, you can name as many backups as you like in your Health Care Proxy document.

- Members could collectively contribute funds to hire a professional—such as an elder law attorney or geriatric care manager—to serve as the final backup. This professional can act as a guide, help the group navigate challenges, and meet with the group once or twice a year to maintain a connection.

By showing up for others and forming a network of trusted people, you ensure someone will be there for you when it matters most. "Pay it forward" by supporting others who, in turn, may be more willing to help you.

Hiring a Professional as Your Health Care Proxy

Some people think, "I don't want any of my friends to be my Health Care Proxy. I would rather hire a professional. They can follow my instructions and make sure I am comfortable." Others may not have anyone to act in this role. Whatever the case, some solo seniors need to hire a professional to serve in this role.

Professionals willing to act as Health Care Proxies are often attorneys, social workers, geriatric care managers, or professional fiduciaries. California, Arizona, Oregon, and Nevada have a regulated professional fiduciary designation, requiring training and background checks. Many of these professional fiduciaries are willing to serve as Health Care Proxy. I hope more states follow this model. However, as of the writing of this book, they are the only states I am aware of that provide any oversight for professional fiduciaries.

Unfortunately, finding a professional to serve as your Health Care Proxy can be challenging. As a member of the Massachusetts Chapter of the National Academy of Elder Law Attorneys, I have access to a private online group where we can seek advice. Recently, an attorney posted a question about whether anyone was willing or knew anyone willing to serve as Health Care Proxy for a client who needed a professional in this role. Unfortunately, no one responded to the request. This situation made me realize how challenging it must be for solo seniors to find a trustworthy person to serve as their Health Care Proxy.

Massachusetts requires that an individual serve as the Health Care Proxy. More professionals may be willing to take on this role if a corporation could be named instead of an individual. Having one person bear the responsibility alone makes it challenging to ensure they will always be available to respond, even on weekends or vacations. By allowing a corporation to serve, professionals within the corporation could share this responsibility. The law must change to make this option possible.

If you hire a professional, the professional should have a written agreement explaining their fees. Unfortunately, I am not aware of any state agency, non-profit, or volunteer agency offering professional Health Care Proxy services for free. Perhaps this will change in the future, as it is unfortunate for those with limited resources who have difficulty building a support system.

To help solo seniors find reliable resources and trusted individuals to serve in important roles, I have created a website, www.SoloAllies.com, providing helpful resources and planning tools for solo seniors.

Tips for Hiring a Professional Health Care Proxy

Here are some tips to help you select a professional to serve as your Health Care Proxy:

- Ideally, the person you hire should be local.

- Try to select someone younger than you who does not work alone. It is best to have a backup plan in case they become unavailable.

- Ask if they have a succession plan in place. It should not be a deal-breaker, as no one can guarantee they will be able to fulfill this role forever. Having a plan for the time being is more important than a perfect one. If necessary, you can always change it later.

- The person should ask about your preferences and wishes and record this information for future reference so they can honor your wishes if they need to make a decision for you.

- If there is a crisis, you will rely on that person to be there for you, so make sure you trust and like them.

Please don't execute a Health Care Proxy document, put it in a drawer, and realize that you haven't talked to the attorney or social worker you chose in ten years. I recommend you review your documents each year and check in with your chosen Health Care Proxy to ensure they are still available to assist you. Choosing the right person as your Health Care Proxy ensures that your wishes and medical preferences are honored when you cannot advocate for yourself. This person's commitment to being there for you in your time of need is invaluable.

Sharing the Health Care Proxy Document

A Health Care Proxy is useless if no one knows it exists or where to find it. To ensure that the right people have access to the document when you need it:

- Make sure your doctor has a copy of your Health Care Proxy document and ask to include it in your medical record.

- Give a copy to the person you are appointing.

- Ask your attorney to keep a copy on file.

- Make sure that a friend or neighbor knows how to contact your Health Care Proxy so they can let them know in an emergency.

If no one can find your Health Care Proxy and your other estate planning documents, then Guardianship will be necessary. In Chapter 8, you will find suggestions about updating and storing these documents so they are ready when needed. You will also find a helpful Emergency Contact and Important Information organizer at the end of this book.

The following frequently asked questions will help you better understand the importance of the Health Care Proxy:

Common Questions About the Health Care Proxy

How much control does my Health Care Proxy have?

If you cannot communicate or make decisions for yourself, the person you designate as your Health Care Proxy will decide what medical treatments you should have. They may make decisions about dialysis, feeding tubes, blood transfusions, surgery, ventilation, and other life-prolonging options.

However, if you regain your ability to communicate and understand, the person no longer makes decisions for you. For example, if you were in a coma but woke up, you would make decisions for yourself again.

There may be differences from state to state, but in Massachusetts, the Health Care Proxy can make whatever decisions they choose. The document does not provide specific instructions for the designated person to follow. Therefore, you should have a conversation with them about your general wishes for medical treatment if you were ever in a situation where your quality of life was significantly impaired and you were not expected to recover. You should also execute an Advanced Directive, which we will discuss in the next chapter, to provide written guidance about your treatment preferences.

Can I change my Health Care Proxy?

You can change or revoke your Health Care Proxy at any time. You must complete a new document or formally revoke the existing one. If you revoke it but appear incompetent, someone will likely intervene and file a petition for Guardianship.

Do I need a lawyer to create a Health Care Proxy?

Some states provide standard forms that you can fill out, which are usually straightforward. While using a lawyer is not necessary, a lawyer will ensure the document is valid in your state.

Is a Health Care Proxy document legally binding?

A Health Care Proxy is legally binding if it complies with your state's laws and regulations.

What happens if I don't have a Health Care Proxy?

If the person cannot make decisions for themselves, Guard-ianship becomes necessary when a person does not have a Health Care Proxy. A hospital, social service, or government agent will likely intervene and file a Guardianship petition.

• • • •

I want to empower you to take control of your future so your wishes will be respected. A Health Care Proxy is essential if you cannot speak for yourself. Choose a reliable individual or professional, keep your document updated, and ensure it is accessible. By planning ahead, you will have peace of mind and maintain control over your medical care.

3. HEALTH CARE DIRECTIVES

"The best way to predict the future is to create it."
— *Abraham Lincoln*

A Health Care Proxy protects you from being placed under Guardianship by appointing someone you trust to make health care decisions if you cannot make them yourself. Communicating your wishes to that person is critical, but what if you wanted to be more specific? In this chapter, I look at the additional documents you can put in place to guide the person's decisions and give you peace of mind.

These documents fall under the broad category of "Health Care Directives." They are never a substitute for a Health Care Proxy. Think of these documents as "the icing on the cake." They are great, but the Health Care Proxy is the foundation.

"Advanced Directive" is an umbrella term for a document describing the type of treatment or medical care you want to receive in certain circumstances involving end-of-life decision-making. One case illustrating the importance of a well-prepared Advanced Directive involves Maria, who appointed her friend as her Health Care Proxy.

Maria

Unfortunately, when Maria needed help, the friend she had appointed to act as her Health Care Proxy could not help her. The hospital went to court to appoint a Guardian for Maria. Maria had a detailed Advanced Directive outlining her end-of-life care wishes, specifically stating that she did not want to be on a ventilator or have CPR performed on her if she went into cardiac arrest. The lawyer, acting as her Guardian, presented this Advanced Directive to the court to seek a court order to allow her to make end-of-life care decisions aligned with her documented wishes. Although Advanced Directives are not legally binding in Massachusetts, the court relied heavily on the document to guide its decision, ensuring that Maria's desires were honored, allowing her to go on hospice and receive comfort measures only at the end of her life.

This case shows how important an Advanced Directive can be in safeguarding your wishes, even when unforeseen circumstances arise, and your designated Health Care Proxy cannot act.

The Advanced Directive

An Advanced Directive is a legal document that outlines your medical care preferences if you cannot communicate or make decisions for yourself. It typically includes instructions about treatments, such as life support or resuscitation. It may also be called a "Living Will."

You may create an Advanced Directive, in addition to the Health Care Proxy, to provide more detailed, written instructions about end-of-life decision-making. However, in many states, an Advanced Directive is not legally binding. This means that your Health Care Proxy does not need to follow it. Nevertheless, it is a valuable reference that informs the person about your wishes, allowing them to make decisions that align with your values and preferences. It also makes the decision more manageable and less emotionally draining for your Health Care Proxy when they know they are following your wishes.

The Advanced Directive can cover various medical decisions, including preferences for life-sustaining treatments, pain management, and other end-of-life care options. Creating an Advanced Directive involves thoughtful consideration of your values and may include discussions with your health care providers. It is important to review and update your Advanced Directive to reflect any changes in your wishes or medical condition.

How to Create an Advanced Directive

There are several ways you can create an Advanced Directive:

1. **Write Your Own:** If you decide to write your own, make sure it clearly states your medical preferences and is signed by two witnesses. If you live in a state that recognizes Advanced Directives as legally binding, you must ensure that the document meets your state's legal requirements. Ask the following questions to guide you in preparing your Advanced Directive:

   - What kind of medical treatments do you want or not want if you are seriously ill or injured?

   - Under what conditions would you want to stop receiving treatment?

   - Would your wishes change if the illness or injury caused physical versus mental impairment?

   - What are your thoughts on quality of life versus life-sustaining treatments?

2. **Online Options:** Many online resources can help you create an Advanced Directive. The "Do It Yourself Estate Planning" documents on www.SoloAllies.com include an Advanced Directive.

3. **Seek Assistance from Health Care Providers:** Doctors, social workers, or hospital staff may be able to help you create an Advanced Directive.

4. **Community Resources:** Many communities offer workshops or resources to help individuals create Advanced Directives. For assistance and information, check with

local senior centers, legal aid societies, or community health organizations.

5. **Meet With an Attorney:** Consulting with an Elder Law or Estate Planning attorney can ensure that your Advanced Directive is comprehensive and legally sound, especially if you live in a state where these documents are legally binding. An attorney will provide personalized advice and help tailor the document to your needs and circumstances.

In addition to the Advanced Directive, there are other legal documents and forms that you can put in place to communicate your preferences. They can be a part of an Advanced Directive but also serve as standalone documents depending on your needs and state requirements.

Five Wishes

Created by the non-profit organization Aging with Dignity, Five Wishes is an Advanced Directive designed to be easy to understand and legally valid in many U.S. states. It addresses medical, personal, emotional, and spiritual needs holistically. It includes details about medical decisions and end-of-life care, such as ways to help you feel comfortable, cared for, and at peace. It cannot replace the Health Care Proxy document. Still, it provides guidance and additional information to help your Health Care Proxy honor your wishes. For more information, visit www.fivewishes.org.

Do Not Resuscitate Order (DNR)

A DNR is a legal document that instructs medical providers and first responders that if your heart stops or you stop breathing, they should not attempt to revive you.

DNRs are usually only appropriate for frail patients for whom it doesn't make sense to administer CPR. I have had some elderly clients who taped their DNRs to their refrigerators so the paramedics would see them in an emergency. If you want to sign a DNR Order, speak to your doctor. The process generally involves meeting with your doctor, who will want to ensure you fully understand the implications of signing it and include it in your medical record. DNRs should be reviewed periodically and updated, especially if health changes occur. DNR laws vary from state to state, and many jurisdictions have specific forms for EMTs to recognize and honor the order.

POLST

A POLST (Physician Orders for Life-Sustaining Treatment) is a medical order designed for individuals with serious illnesses or advanced age. It provides clear instructions on the types of life-sustaining treatments you want or do not want.

The key areas that a POLST Order covers are:

- **CPR (Cardiopulmonary Resuscitation) Orders:** These specify whether the patient wants CPR if their heart stops.

- **Medical Interventions or Treatment Scope:** Defines the extent of medical care you want, such as:

  - Full treatment, including mechanical ventilation, intubation, and ICU care.

  - Selective treatment may involve non-invasive support such as oxygen therapy, antibiotics, or intravenous fluids but avoids aggressive interventions like ventilators.

  - Comfort-focused care prioritizes pain relief and symptom management, such as administering morphine, without hospital transfers or life-prolonging treatments.

  - Artificial Nutrition and Hydration: Details preferences for feeding and hydration, including long term tube feeding or refusing artificial nutrition to allow natural progression.

- Other Life-Sustaining Treatments: Includes options like dialysis, blood transfusions, or other advanced treatments.

- **Location of Care Preferences:** Specifies where you want to receive care, such as staying at home or avoiding ICU care, to ensure comfort and dignity during treatment.

Unlike an Advanced Directive, which serves as a general guide, a POLST Order is legally binding once signed by both the patient and a health care provider. However, its enforceability may vary depending on where you live, as each state has specific regulations and procedures.

POLST forms are available in most states. They are also referred to as Medical Orders for Life-Sustaining Treatment (MOLST), Medical Orders for Scope of Treatment (MOST), or Physician Orders for Scope of Treatment (POST). Your doctor can provide the form to you and help you complete it. You do not need a lawyer to create a POLST Order.

However, you must still have a Health Care Proxy in place, as you need an actual person to be involved with medical decision-making if you cannot. As always, it is important to regularly review and update the form your wishes or medical condition change.

• • • •

While a Health Care Proxy document forms the foundation, additional documents such as Advanced Directives, Living Wills, POLSTs, and DNRs provide further information about your wishes, ensuring your treatment preferences are honored. While some may not be legally binding in every state, they help guide health care providers and loved ones. Thoughtful planning offers peace of mind and dignity, helping you confidently face the future.

4. PLANNING FOR EMERGENCIES: THE DURABLE POWER OF ATTORNEY

"Let our advance worrying become advance thinking and planning." — *Winston Churchill*

In addition to the Health Care Proxy, the Power of Attorney is another key legal document everyone should have, especially solo seniors, to prepare for emergencies or the unexpected. This chapter focuses on the importance of the Power of Attorney. A Power of Attorney allows someone to handle your finances if you get sick or hurt and cannot handle it yourself. Without this, banks, financial institutions, and the IRS won't give anyone access to your accounts.

Jane's story illustrates the importance of having a Durable Power of Attorney:

Jane's Story

Jane was a fiercely independent woman who lived alone since her husband passed away many years ago. She prided herself on managing her finances and household without any help. However, one day, she suffered a stroke and was rushed to the hospital. Although she survived, the stroke left her unable to speak or communicate clearly.

As the days passed, Jane's bills began to pile up. Her mortgage, utility bills, and credit card payments were all due, but no one had access to her accounts to pay them. Jane's niece, Sarah, who lived in another state, wanted to help. However, when she contacted Jane's bank, they refused to speak with her. The bank informed Sarah that without a Power of Attorney, they could not grant her access to Jane's accounts. Sarah was frustrated, knowing that Jane's finances were deteriorating while she could not do anything about it.

Eventually, Sarah had to ask the court to appoint her as Jane's Conservator. This process took several months and required expensive legal fees. During that time, Jane's credit suffered, and the bank threatened to foreclose her home. Jane could have avoided this if she signed a Durable Power of Attorney before her stroke.

The Durable Power of Attorney

A Power of Attorney (POA) is a legal document that allows a person to act on your behalf for legal or financial matters. A Power of Attorney can be temporary or "durable," meaning it remains in effect if you become permanently incapacitated. Depending on its scope, it can cover various matters, such as managing bank accounts, paying bills, filing tax returns, making real estate and investment transactions, and business decisions.

There are different types of Power of Attorney documents, each serving a different purpose:

A Limited Power of Attorney grants specific authority to handle a task for a short time. For example, if you were buying a house but could not attend the closing meeting, you would provide a Limited Power of Attorney to your attorney, allowing them to sign the documents for you that day.

The Durable Power of Attorney is used for long term planning. This is the type of Power of Attorney document to use when planning for your future to ensure that someone can take care of your finances if you cannot. Durable means you need the document to remain in effect even if you become incapacitated. Since this is the whole point of executing it, please make sure there is language in the Power of Attorney document mentioning that it survives incapacity or is durable. The Durable Power of Attorney is often called simply the Power of Attorney. Throughout this book, when I refer to a Power of Attorney, I am referencing a Durable Power of Attorney.

There is an important thing you need to understand about this document: When you sign a Power of Attorney, it usually goes into effect immediately upon signing, but the understanding is that it would only be used if you need help in the future. You might be thinking, "As long as I can still handle my affairs, why should they be able to act right now?" The main reason for this immediate authority is to ensure that your agent can act without delay if needed. If their ability to act only begins when you cannot act for yourself, financial institutions may require an order from the court to allow your agent to help. This would cause a significant delay at a time when you need help immediately.

Suppose you don't feel comfortable giving someone authority now, even with the understanding that they would not act unless needed. In that case, there are two options to consider:

- **A Springing Power of Attorney:** This document includes instructions that allow your agent to act only if a doctor certifies in writing that you are incapacitated. While that sounds ideal, this type of Power of Attorney can create challenges. For instance, financial institutions or your bank may require that your agent obtain a court order to prove you cannot manage your affairs before allowing them to access your account. This could defeat the purpose of having the Power of Attorney, delay access to your accounts for weeks or months, and result in the need for Guardianship or Conservatorship.

- **Hold the document in escrow:** Another option is to ask someone you trust to hold the Power of Attorney document and only release it to your agent if you become incapacitated. For example, if you appoint a friend, you could ask your attorney to hold the document and provide instructions on when they should release the Power of Attorney document to your friend, like receiving valid proof that you cannot handle your affairs. In this scenario, you could also ask your friend to call your attorney if you become incapacitated or need more help managing your financial affairs.

Ultimately, you want the Power of Attorney to work when you need it, and you want to avoid the additional step of having the court determine that you are incapacitated.

Powers to Include in the Durable Power of Attorney

Most Power of Attorney documents are created to cover unforeseen circumstances. They typically include broad powers so that, whatever situation arises, the appointed person can help you without obtaining a Conservatorship. Be sure to read the document and ensure you are comfortable with each of the powers you grant.

There are certain powers that I recommend solo seniors include in the Power of Attorney, including:

- **The Power of Substitution:** This power allows your agent to choose someone to act in their place if they cannot. Since you have no way of knowing what might be happening in their life, when you might need them, having this power included in the document provides flexibility if it is a bad time for them. It will give them the option of choosing someone else to act in their place.

- **The Power to Make Gifts to a Trust for Your Benefit:** Sometimes trusts are recommended for Medicaid or Estate Tax planning, and gifting power is needed. In order for your agent to gift money to a Trust, this power must be included in the Power of Attorney document.

- **The Power to Buy/Sell/Mortgage Real Estate:** Without this power, your agent won't be able to buy, sell, or obtain a mortgage for your real estate.

Tips for Choosing Someone to Act as Your Power of Attorney

Deciding who to choose to act as your Power of Attorney, can be difficult. Here are some tips to help you decide:

- The ideal person should be organized, reliable, and preferably local. Trustworthiness is crucial since the Power of Attorney can be misused in the wrong hands, making it a "license to steal."

- Serving as a Power of Attorney requires significant effort and is like a part-time job. The individual in this role must be responsible, willing, and capable of fulfilling their duties. In many cases, asking a friend to take on this responsibility can feel like a burden.

- A trusted family member who is organized, capable, and good with finances is often the best choice for this role. However, many solo seniors do not have anyone fitting this description to rely on. Friends or neighbors typically are not ideal options, as the responsibilities can be overwhelming. Sadly, many solo seniors don't have anyone to rely upon. If this is the case, hiring a professional may be the best option.

- When in doubt, appoint a professional as a back up to your friend or family member.

The Importance of Asking First: Kathy's Story

I received a call from a woman named Sarah. Her friend, Kathy, had named her Power of Attorney but never told Sarah about this. Unfortunately, Kathy had dementia and needed nursing home care. When Sarah learned she was responsible, she tried her best but quickly became overwhelmed. The job required far more time and effort than she could handle.

To make matters worse, her husband was also sick, and it was just too much to take on. Sarah felt terrible about not being able to help her friend. She could not handle the stress of managing Kathy's finances and her vacant home during the winter months.

Sarah called my office, asking for help. Since no one else was named in the document and it did not include a Power of Substitution, the only way to resolve it involved going to court to appoint a Conservator for Kathy. We represented Sarah in the Conservatorship petition. The court appointed a stranger, an attorney Kathy had never met, to get involved and manage her financial affairs. Had Kathy asked Sarah first and named a professional as a backup, or included a Power of Substitution in the document, she would not have put her friend in such a difficult position.

Get Organized

If you do need help from your Power of Attorney, they will have a much easier job, if you are prepared and organized. The more you can do now to organize your finances, set up automatic payments and withdraws, and simplify your accounts, the easier it will be if someone needs to step in to help. Here are a few tips to help you prepare:

- Provide your Power of Attorney with a list of your assets and update it each year to ensure they are prepared to act on your behalf. The Solo Senior Organizer, at the end of this book, is a good tool to get started. If you don't feel comfortable sharing this information now, make sure that they know how to find it if it is needed, or that a professional you are working with, such as your attorney or financial advisor, has this information and can share it with them at that time.

- If you want your Power of Attorney to have access to your home, provide them with a key or let them know how to access one. Be sure to inform them of any valuables or special instructions.

- Some financial institutions, like Vanguard and Fidelity, have their own Power of Attorney forms you must fill out. Check with your financial institutions to ask if they have specific forms you should complete to ensure they recognize the Power of Attorney.

Common Questions
About the Durable Power of Attorney

How long does the Durable Power of Attorney last?

The Durable Power of Attorney is only valid during your life. All power to act ends upon death.

Can I change my Power of Attorney?

You can revoke your Power of Attorney by notifying the person you appointed and any financial institution where you have an account.

How can I add safeguards to my Power of Attorney?

When drafting a Power of Attorney, you can safeguard your interests by establishing a system of checks and balances. Here are some things to consider:

If you own real estate, you can include a clause in your Power of Attorney document requiring the agent to obtain written consent from a specific person before selling it.

You can draft a second Power of Attorney that grants authority to a trusted friend or another attorney to oversee the person acting as your Power of Attorney. You may authorize someone to request an accounting of any funds your Power of Attorney

---

handles. Most attorneys have malpractice insurance, and some professional fiduciaries are bonded, meaning that their insurance provides a guarantee against financial loss due to dishonesty, failure to perform, or other reasons. These things protect you.

Do I need a lawyer to create a Durable Power of Attorney?

No, although recommended, you do not need an estate planning or elder law attorney to draft your Durable Power of Attorney. A generic form may not include important language. For example, as mentioned earlier, the power of substitution and, in some instances, the power of gifting can be important. Attorneys, especially elder law attorneys, will discuss your unique situation and can tailor the document to your needs to provide flexibility and avoid court involvement.

Please visit www.SoloAllies.com for planning documents and resources designed specifically for solo seniors. This website offers a do-it-yourself option for legal documents tailored to solo seniors living in Massachusetts and plans to expand to other states. It also helps to connect you with elder law and estate planning attorneys experienced with helping solo seniors.

What happens if I don't have a Durable Power of Attorney?

If you don't have a Durable Power of Attorney document or it cannot be found, the court must appoint a Conservator to manage your legal and financial affairs.

• • • •

There is no shame in not having everything figured out or a person you can trust to count on. By consulting with an elder law attorney, executing a Durable Power of Attorney, and identifying people you can count on, you will have taken significant steps toward safeguarding your future, preparing for unforeseen circumstances, and having peace of mind.

5. SECURING YOUR LEGACY: LAST WILL AND TESTAMENT AND REVOCABLE TRUST

"For we brought nothing into the world,
and we can take nothing out." — 1 Timothy 6:7

As we age, we start thinking about how we want to be remembered and our impact on the world. Some want their legacy to live on by giving to charities, schools, or causes they believe in, spreading kindness and generosity far beyond their lifetime. One such example is Sylvia Bloom.

Sylvia Bloom

Sylvia grew up in Brooklyn during the Great Depression. She worked hard to put herself through school and earn a college degree. After graduating, she worked as a legal secretary for 67 years, dying in 2016, shortly after her retirement, at 96.

She lived a simple, unassuming life, and along the way, she made some very smart investments, amassing an estate worth over $8 million. She left some money to her nieces and nephews, but she gave the bulk of her estate, $6.2 million, to the Henry Street Settlement in New York City to provide scholarships for students in need to attend college. It was the largest gift the charity had ever received, and the organization was very thankful. Sylvia's generous gift will make a tremendous difference in the lives of many young people who may not have been able to go to college otherwise.

Giving millions of dollars to charity may not be possible, but any donation is valuable and likely to be appreciated. Contributing to charity can positively impact the world and create a meaningful legacy.

In this chapter, I will discuss the two legal documents that ensure that your assets and belongings will go to the people and organizations you want to receive these things at the end of your life: the Last Will and Testament and the Revocable Trust.

The Last Will and Testament

A Last Will and Testament is a legal document describing how you wish to distribute your assets upon death. Although requirements vary by state, a Will must be in writing, signed by you, and witnessed by at least two other people. Your Will should include several important pieces of information.

Your Will should clearly describe who you want to give your property to at the end of your life. Suppose you have specific items or assets that you wish to leave to certain charities or people. In that case, it should identify these items or financial assets. However, when creating a Will, describing everything you own is unnecessary. It is often easier to refer to "your residuary estate," which means anything you own when you die that is not already specifically identified or described in the Will.

Choosing an Executor

In your Will, you need to decide who should manage your estate. This person is called the "Personal Representative" or "Executor." Once the court appoints the person, they pay all outstanding debts and taxes and distribute the remaining property to the people or charities named in your Will.

Your Will should include a list of generous powers authorizing your Executor to have the authority to take specific actions without requiring them to obtain a court order. For example, the power to sell or mortgage real estate is important, as without this, your Executor will need to get an order from the court allowing them to do this, which will be costly and time-consuming.

Other important powers include the ability to collect any debts owed to you, to sue, to open and close bank accounts, to distribute money to any children who are under 18 in a specific way, to hire professionals to help them, and to allow them to pay themselves a reasonable fee for the work that they are doing as your Executor.

Make sure that the person you choose is responsible, organized, and trustworthy. Serving as the Executor is a big job and a significant time commitment. It may be difficult for someone to take on this role if they have a busy life or don't live near you. Most people don't understand how complicated this job can be.

I often meet with clients who choose a friend or family member they like, thinking this is a compliment and honor to the person. In reality, they are burdening them with a job that involves considerable time, energy, and stress. This may be appropriate if you leave them significant assets or money in your Will. However, if you plan to leave everything to charity, it will likely be an annoyance to a friend to take on this role. You should talk to the person you wish to appoint and ensure they are up to the task.

For some clients, this decision is so hard that it prevents them from creating a Will, which is even worse. Many Elder Law and Estate Planning attorneys are willing to serve as Executor. They are often the best choice, as they know how to do this efficiently. To find attorneys near you who may be willing to help, visit www.SoloAllies.com.

It is very important to remember that your Will controls assets solely in your name at the time of death. In other words, it does not control assets you own jointly with others, accounts that name Beneficiaries, or accounts in the name of a Trust. These accounts will go to the person named as the Joint Owner, Beneficiary, or Trustee.

I was involved in a case of a woman who named her friend on her checking account for convenience so that she could help her pay bills. In her Will, she wanted her estate to go to charities. After her death, the checking account, which was jointly held with her friend, went to the friend and not the charities. It was unclear what her intention had been. To ensure your wishes will be honored, you must know how your accounts are titled and review your beneficiary designations.

The Probate Process

Before anyone can access your assets, your Will must go through an extra step called "Probate."

Probate is the legal process of giving your Executor the authority to access your accounts and retitle your assets. Retitling means changing the ownership of assets from your own name to the name of your estate so that the Executor can pay your debts and expenses and distribute your assets according to your wishes.

There are several steps in the Probate process. These are:

1. The Executor named in the Will or an interested party files a request with the court to approve the Will. A judge must ensure that the Will was executed correctly and is valid.

2. The closest blood relatives and anyone included in your Will must receive legal notice that the Executor (or Personal Representative) filed the Will with the court. If they wish to object, they must do so by a specific date.

3. If there are no objections, the court will appoint the Executor named in the Will to handle the estate.

4. Once the Executor is appointed, the person must collect your assets and close your financial accounts. They must open a new bank account for the estate, pay the debts and taxes, and distribute the assets according to your Will.

5. Sometimes, the Executor must file an account of how they handled the money in the estate. The court oversees the Executor's actions.

In most states, the Probate process is relatively painless. You won't ever need to deal with the Probate of your own estate since you will no longer be alive. If you do not hire a professional Executor, the friend or family member you choose will likely hire an attorney to assist them.

Dying Without a Will — Intestate

If a person dies without a Will, they are said to have died "Intestate"—the legal term for "no Will." Probate is still necessary and can be more complicated than if a person died with a Will.

Often, people can't decide to whom they want to leave their property, so they do nothing. What happens then? If you don't have a Will, your assets will be divided among your closest living blood relatives. Maybe you have first cousins you rarely see or second cousins you have never met. They will receive your assets. Is this what you want? If not, you should name a person or charity as the beneficiary of your estate as soon as possible. The closest living blood relatives may request to be appointed Executor. If no known relatives exist, a Public Administrator may file the petition.

In most states, each county has a few Public Administrators appointed by the Governor or another authority to act in this role. Once appointed, the Public Administrator will pay the debts and expenses of the estate. Creditors have up to one year from death to file a claim against the estate. After that time, the remaining funds will be distributed according to state laws, typically to the closest blood relatives. If there are no known relatives, the state that you live in will normally hold the money as abandoned property.

For 15 years, I served as a Public Administrator in Boston (Suffolk County), Massachusetts. I was the stranger who showed up to handle estates of those who failed to plan and had no family. Of all the cases I have been involved in, one of the saddest was Joe's.

Joe

The court appointed me as Public Administrator for Joe's estate. He was in his 70s and died in his home. No one discovered that he died for months, and his body decomposed in his home. The Medical Examiner contacted me to ask me if I was willing to take the case, as his body had been sitting unclaimed in the morgue for months.

As Public Administrator, I collect the estate's assets and determine if there are any relatives, pay the debts and taxes, and distribute any remaining funds to the closest living blood relatives. If I can't find any heirs, I turn the money over to the Treasurer of the Commonwealth of Massachusetts, who holds the funds in unclaimed property. In Joe's case, he had several first cousins, many of whom he never knew. They received his assets.

Usually, when I found heirs, they were distant relatives who never even knew the person. Since we live in a world full of scams, the heirs were often understandably skeptical of believing me when I first contacted them to notify them that they were heirs. Yet, they were always pleasantly surprised to get unexpected money.

I had one fascinating case when—just as I was about to distribute the funds to the heirs— I received a call from a niece explaining that the woman who died had a baby, but it was a family secret. After looking into it, she was correct. That baby was now an adult woman who nuns had raised. Since she was never officially adopted, she was entitled to the funds from her mother's estate, not the nieces and nephews. The nieces and nephews were disappointed to lose what they thought they would receive. Still, the daughter was very happy that I found her and that she received something from her mother's estate.

Although I found this case interesting, you don't want to rely on a total stranger at the end of your life to try to locate relatives you never met or dig up family secrets.

The Revocable Trust

A Will is a necessary part of estate planning. Some solo seniors should also consider creating a Revocable Trust. A Revocable Trust is an extra, meaning it is a document you create in addition to a Will. As we have seen, a Will must go through Probate, which can be time-consuming and costly. If you want to make things easier for those handling your estate, a Revocable Trust, also known as a Living Trust, might be a better option, and is one way to avoid probate.

A Revocable Trust, or Living Trust, is a legal document that allows the person handling your estate to have immediate access to your assets as long as they are titled in the name of your Trust.

Here's why a Revocable Trust is useful in estate planning:

- **Control and flexibility:** If you are alive and mentally capable, you can manage the assets in the Trust just as you would if they were still in your name. You can add or remove assets, change Beneficiaries, or even dissolve the Trust if you wish.

- **Avoiding Probate:** After your death, your Trustee can distribute the assets in the Trust to your beneficiaries without going through Probate. They can receive their inheritance more quickly and with less hassle. It also makes it easier for the person handling your assets to do their job.

- **Flexibility:** A Trust allows you to dictate what happens to your assets even after death. For example, you might want to leave money or property to someone to use while they are alive, but when they die, you want it to go to another person or charity. A Trust allows you to do this, but a Will does not. Another example may be that you may only want to leave something to someone if they meet certain conditions, such as being drug-free or finishing college. A Trust will give you the flexibility to do this, and it is much more difficult with only a Will.

- **Privacy:** Unlike a Will, which becomes a public record during Probate, a Trust is private. The details of your estate and the distribution of your assets remain confidential.

- **Incapacity planning:** If you become incapacitated and unable to manage your affairs, the Trustee (a person or institution you designate) can step in and manage the Trust assets on your behalf, according to the instructions in the Trust document. It avoids the need for a court-appointed Guardian or Conservator.

- **Continuity:** A Revocable Trust provides a smooth transition of asset management from you to your Trustee and Beneficiaries, ensuring that your financial matters are handled according to your wishes.

If you create a Revocable Trust, your Will is only used if you have assets in your name alone when you die. Most attorneys recommend creating a Will in addition to a Revocable Trust. None of us know exactly what we will own at the time of our death. Sometimes, people are entitled to refunds or assets they did not expect after they die, and then the Will is important.

Do You Need a Revocable Trust?

A Revocable Trust is not necessary, but in some situations, it is the best way to help you ensure your wishes are honored. Ask yourself these questions to help determine whether you need a Revocable Trust:

- Do you want to leave your assets to children who are under 18 years old?

- Are you in a second marriage, with children from a prior marriage?

- Are you concerned about your privacy?

- Do you want to include what are called "Conditional Gifts"? Conditional Gifting means that certain conditions must be met before the person can receive their inheritance. For example, the person must graduate from college before they will receive their gift.

- Do you want to give property or assets to someone for a certain period of time or just for their life, but then you want to decide what happens to the property after they die?

- Do you wish to avoid the Probate process?

- Do you want to make things as easy as possible for the person handling your estate?

If you answered "yes" to any of the above questions, I recommend you talk to an attorney about establishing a Revocable Trust.

"Funding the Trust" to Avoid Probate

Creating a Revocable Trust is a powerful tool for estate planning, but it only works if you properly "fund" the Trust. This process involves transferring ownership (the title) of your assets, such as real estate, bank accounts, and investments, into the name of the Trust while you are still alive. Without this critical step, your assets may still need to go through the probate process, even if you have a Trust in place.

Here are ways you can "fund" a Revocable Trust:

1. **Retitle Your Assets:** Here is some advice on how you can change the title of your assets:

   • **Real Estate:** You may need an attorney to draft and record a new deed transferring your property to the Trust. This ensures that your real estate avoids Probate and the property is added to your Trust while you are alive.

   • **Bank and Investment Accounts:** Contact your banks or financial institutions to change the title on your account from your name to the name of your Trust. You will need to provide a copy of the Trust. When the Trust is revocable, you can continue using your Social Security number for this account, which should not impact your income taxes.

   • **Vehicles:** If allowed in your state, retitle your cars in the Trust's name by visiting your local DMV. This is often not worth doing unless the vehicle is very valuable. You should check with your auto insurance company to ensure it won't cause a problem or increase your premium rates.

2. **Update Beneficiary Designations:** You may also name the Trust as the beneficiary of financial accounts or life

insurance. However, you must be careful and thoughtful when dealing with tax-deferred retirement accounts. With this type of account, it is better to name specific people than the Trust to minimize income tax consequences for your beneficiaries, unless you leave everything to charity.

3. **Transfer Personal Property:** You can create a document that assigns ownership to the Trust for significant assets like jewelry or artwork. This document should be signed, dated, and kept with your trust records.

As you acquire new assets, make sure you change the name of these assets into the Trust. By carefully funding your Trust, you ensure that your assets are managed according to your wishes, avoiding the delays and costs associated with Probate. This step is essential for making the most of your estate planning and securing the legacy you wish to leave behind; without it, your estate will likely need to go through Probate.

Considering Whether to Appoint a Co-Trustee

A Trustee is the person or organization that manages the assets in a Trust. If you are alive and capable, you will be the Trustee of your Trust. Usually, you will be the sole Trustee, which means that you are the only person managing your Trust while you are alive and able to do so.

However, in some situations, people wish to appoint someone as a Co-Trustee. This means you and a Co-Trustee are appointed to manage the Trust together. A Co-Trustee can provide additional support, which can be helpful if you need assistance now or soon. It may be a good idea for someone with a serious diagnosis or who knows they will need help.

However, it also means that you and your Co-Trustee must agree on decisions regarding the Trust. If you add a Co-Trustee, you may want to include a provision in the Trust that you, as the Donor of the Trust, have the power to remove them. It may also be a good way to see how your Co-Trustee handles the job and ensure they are up for it.

You will always choose someone to act as a Successor Trustee. They will step in if you are incapacitated or at the end of your life and manage the Trust then.

Choosing a Successor Trustee

If you have created a Trust for your estate, you will serve as Trustee while you are alive. You will have full access to the assets and money included in the Trust for whatever you may want or need in life. It's important to decide who will act as your Successor Trustee. This person will take charge of the Trust if you become incapacitated or die.

The role of a Successor Trustee is similar to an Executor or Personal Representative of a Will. However, unlike an Executor, a Trustee's actions are not overseen by the court unless a problem arises. Therefore, it's crucial to choose someone trustworthy. Ideally, this person should have experience acting as a Trustee or be willing to hire an attorney for advice.

Professionals like attorneys, banks, and accountants may also be willing to serve in this role and offer the benefit of experience.

Consider Adding a Trust Protector

Including a Trust Protector in your Revocable Trust can add an extra layer of security and oversight.

A Trust Protector is an independent third party with the authority to monitor and supervise the Successor Trustee's actions, ensuring they are in the Trust's and its Beneficiaries' best interest.

A Trust Protector could be a younger friend or relative. You may not want to burden them with managing the day-to-day tasks, but you want them to check on the Trustee to ensure they are doing a good job. They can step in and even replace the Trustee if they see any mismanagement.

Common Questions About Wills and Revocable Trusts

Can I write my own Will?

You can write your own Will, but it's better to seek legal advice to ensure it meets legal requirements, accurately reflects your wishes, and is executed according to state laws. One small mistake or omission may result in a complicated court process. If you are interested in doing this yourself, please visit www.SoloAllies.com for DIY legal forms created specifically to help solo seniors. At the time of writing this book, these forms are only available to those in Massachusetts. However, this may expand to other states in the future.

When should I update my Will?

You should update your Will whenever you experience significant life changes, such as marriage, divorce, or a major change in your financial situation. Suppose you wish to make changes after executing your Will. In that case, you must create a new one and sign it properly before witnesses, preferably a notary. Never write on your Will, cross anything off, or make changes. This can cause many problems and result in the need for a trial. The only way to change a will is to have it properly signed and witnessed.

What happens if a Beneficiary in my Will dies before me?

You can include provisions for such situations, such as naming alternate Beneficiaries. If your Will does not provide guidance, state law determines how the Executor distributes the share for the deceased beneficiary. Suppose the person is a close family member, such as a child. In that case, the property will often go to their children, but it depends on the laws in your state and the wording in your Will. It is best to clearly state who you want to receive that person's share if they do not survive you.

Can my Will be challenged?

A family member can challenge your Will, typically claiming undue influence, lack of capacity, or improper execution. Undue influence means that someone exerted pressure on a person to make decisions or sign the Will, making them act in a way they would not have otherwise. Lack of capacity means that the person could not understand the consequences of their actions when signing their Will. Improper execution means that the legal requirements were not followed.

Does a Revocable Trust protect my assets from creditors?

No, because you control the assets, they are still considered part of your estate and not protected from creditors.

Can a Revocable Trust help lower estate taxes?

No, a Revocable Trust does not reduce estate taxes or income taxes.

Can I change or revoke my Revocable Trust?

While alive and capable, you can change or cancel your Trust, as long as it is revocable, at any time by following the procedures outlined in the Trust document, usually by signing an amendment with the changes you want to make or a restatement, which means changing the entire document. You may also revoke the Trust in writing.

When you die, the Trust becomes irrevocable, meaning it can no longer be modified, amended, or revoked. The Successor Trustee takes over and manages the assets according to your instructions. However, it can also become irrevocable if you become incapacitated and are no longer able to manage it. You may also make the Trust irrevocable during your lifetime for specific reasons. However, doing so may have tax consequences, so it is important to consult with an attorney.

• • • •

I have met many clients who feel embarrassed about not having an estate plan. I always reassure them: "You're here now, and that's what matters." I strongly encourage you to create an estate plan. You don't need to be perfectly organized or have everything figured out. In just a few weeks, you can implement a 'good enough' plan for now.

Whether you choose a basic estate plan with a Will or include a Revocable Trust, you will gain peace of mind.

6. SPECIAL CONSIDERATIONS: ADULT CHILDREN THAT NEED HELP AND PETS

"To the world, you may be one person,
but to one person, you may be the world."
— Dr. Seuss

"And God said, I will send them without wings,
so no one suspects they are angels."
— Unknown

This chapter will consider Estate Planning for those with unique circumstances. Some of you may have adult children who, for various reasons, cannot care for themselves or you worry about. Others share your lives with beloved pets, and you want to ensure they are well cared for if something should happen to you. These situations require thoughtful planning and consideration. We will explore the specific strategies and tools you can use to provide for your loved ones, whether they walk on two legs or four.

Planning for Children That Need Help: Supplemental Needs Trust

Many people have children who are unable to take care of themselves. They have often dedicated their lives to caring for their children, even after they reached adulthood. The final act of caring is to plan for when you can no longer be there for them. While it's important to plan for yourself, it's critical to do so if you have a dependent adult child. One story that comes to mind is that of Ruth.

Ruth

Ruth contacted my office from the hospital to prepare her estate plan. I met with her, and we talked about her wishes. Ruth's daughter, a woman in her early 40s, still lived with her. Her daughter had severe anxiety, and Ruth was concerned about her. I recommended that Ruth execute a Will, a Health Care Proxy, a Power of Attorney, and a Supplemental Needs Trust for her adult daughter. Unfortunately, Ruth died right after our initial meeting and before she could execute any documents.

Her daughter, Mary, was left alone, without support. She was anxious, afraid, and agoraphobic. Ruth never had her daughter evaluated, so she was not eligible for public benefits or services. Since Ruth never executed the Trust, the assets she wanted to leave to her daughter would not be protected if Mary needed to qualify for any public benefits.

Mary had no siblings, family, friends, or anyone in her life. When Ruth died, I reached out to Mary to ask if she needed help. She was grateful to have someone help her. I helped Mary arrange her mother's funeral, and Mary and I were the only ones there.

Mary was very anxious. Leaving the house was very difficult for her, even to go to the store, so I arranged for groceries to be delivered. I hired a companion to check on Mary. She continued living at home for a few years. Eventually, her mental illness progressed to the point where it was no longer safe for her to live at home. After repeated psychiatric hospitalizations, the hospital went to court to appoint me as her Guardian. Eventually, Mary moved to an assisted living facility, which was not ideal. Finally, after advocating for years to help her move to a more appropriate setting, she moved to a group home, where she is thriving.

In addition to the essential three documents discussed in previous chapters, if you have an adult child who needs help, it is important to execute a "Supplemental Needs Trust."

A Supplemental Needs Trust preserves the beneficiary's eligibility for government benefits such as Medicaid and Supplemental Security Income (SSI). Because the beneficiary does not own the assets in the Trust, they can remain eligible for benefit programs with an asset limit. Generally, the Trust will supplement government benefits but not replace them. Examples of supplemental needs are costs for companions, cable, cell phones, travel, furniture, cars, gas, and dental or medical expenses not covered by Medicare or Medicaid. Ideally, a parent, family member, or loved one creates it.

The person receiving benefits can establish specific types of Supplemental Needs Trusts using their own money, but these trusts require a "payback provision." These are called "First Party Supplemental Needs Trusts." If the beneficiary is under 65, a "D4A Trust" can be used to protect assets. A Pooled Disability Trust is another type of First-Party Trust used to protect assets, regardless of the beneficiary's age. We will explore the Pooled Disability Trust in greater detail in Chapter 9.

In Mary's situation, as her Guardian, I set up a First Party Supplemental Needs Trust for Mary to protect her inheritance. However, that Trust required a "payback provision" at the end of Mary's life. This means that the money in the Trust won't be considered when determining Mary's eligibility for public benefit programs. At the end of Mary's life, any funds remaining in the Trust must first be paid back to the state for the money they spent on her care. This provision would not have been necessary if Ruth had established a Trust for Mary.

If your child cannot take care of themselves due to medical conditions, if they struggle with mental illness or addiction, consider the following:

- **Get help for your child while you are still alive:** If your child has a mental disability, each state has its equivalent of the Department of Mental Health or the Department of Developmental Services. Contact your state agency to find out how to apply for benefits. Once your child receives benefits, ask the case worker to help you plan for your child and prepare for when you can no longer care for them. It is best to help your child make this change while you are still alive so you can help them adjust. Without a plan, you may leave your child in a dangerous situation.

- **Preserve disability benefits:** If your child is diagnosed with a disability or receives public benefits, a Supplemental Needs Trust allows you to provide financially for your adult child without affecting their eligibility for governmental benefits such as Supplemental Security Income, Medicaid, subsidized housing, or food stamps. The Trustee will use the Trust money to pay for things not covered by public benefits, for example, a cell phone, a car, transportation, legal services, household items/maintenance, furniture, travel, activities, and personal items or services that improve your child's life.

Planning for Children You Worry About Handling Money: The Discretionary Trust

I have met many people who worry about their adult child's (or adult child's spouse's) ability to handle money. They may worry about bankruptcy, divorce, wild spending habits, or recklessness. In this case, having a Will is not enough. Since the child is not disabled, a Supplemental Needs Trust is not necessary. A Discretionary Trust allows you to set the terms and conditions for distributing the assets.

If you have a child struggling with addiction, you should not leave money outright to that child. The money may fuel the addiction. Instead, a parent in this situation can create a Trust for the child. A Trustee (a trusted friend, relative, or attorney) can be appointed to manage the money and decide the amount and frequency of distributions. They can also pay the child's expenses directly. If the child overcomes the addiction or meets certain conditions, you can give the Trustee discretion to terminate the Trust.

A Discretionary Trust allows you to appoint a Trustee, someone other than your child, who will manage the assets in the Trust. The Trustee has full discretion over when and how much money is distributed to your child. This Trust is beneficial if you worry that an outright inheritance might be mismanaged, wasted, or misused. For instance, if your child struggles with addiction or has a spouse prone to overspending, a Discretionary Trust provides a safeguard. The Trustee can directly pay for your child's expenses (such as rent, health care, or education) rather than giving your child full control over the funds.

Planning for Pets: The Pet Trust

Do you lie awake at night wondering what would happen to your pet if you could not care for them?

While you can't leave property directly to a pet, you can name a Caretaker in your Will and leave that person money to care for your pet. However, there is no guarantee that they will fulfill your wishes and no ongoing oversight.

In some states, you can set up a "Pet Trust."

A Pet Trust is a legal arrangement to care for a pet after its owner dies or becomes incapacitated. It stipulates that a Trustee will hold property (cash, for example) "in trust" for the animal's benefit. The money in the Pet Trust can pay for caregivers, medical treatment, and whatever is possible to ensure your pet has a good quality of life.

If you are ever temporarily incapacitated, you should also provide the person you choose as your Power of Attorney with instructions and information about your pet. Consider the following story:

Laura

I was involved in a case where a woman was hospitalized. Her house was in deplorable condition, and it was unsafe to enter it. She asked me to feed her cat, who was still in the home, without food for weeks. Considering it was not safe to enter the house, I would leave food just inside the front door for the cat each day.

The cat was shy and was hiding in the house. Since it was unsafe to enter the house, I did not know what to do. I contacted Animal Control, who gave me a humane trap to capture the cat, leaving the trap just inside the front door. I left food inside the trap, and eventually, after a few days, the cat was safely in the trap, and I brought him to the vet. Eventually, Laura moved into an assisted-living facility, which allowed cats, and they were reunited.

Had Laura made provisions for her cat in the case of an emergency, it would not have gone hungry for weeks before I stepped in to help.

Establishing a Pet Trust

A famous legal case of a Pet Trust was that of American hotelier and real estate investor Leona Helmsley, known as the "Queen of Mean."

Leona Helmsley

In her Will, Leona Helmsley left $12 million to care for her beloved Maltese dog, Trouble. She gave more money to Trouble's Pet Trust than some family members. This led to a legal battle, and eventually, the court cut Trouble's Trust Fund down to $2 million and increased the family's inheritance.

It is hard to imagine how any pet would ever need that much money. But, being a rich dog has downsides, as poor Trouble faced kidnapping and death threats. He needed a security guard to keep him safe. In the end, he was well cared for until he died at age 12.

A Pet Trust helps ensure your pet is cared for its entire life. However, it is very different from other Trusts because the beneficiary, your pet, cannot make their wishes known or let someone know if they are not being properly cared for. Therefore, you must choose trustworthy people to look out for and take care of your pet, specifically in the following three roles:

- **Trustee:** The Trustee manages and uses the Pet Trust money for your pet's needs. If needed, they pay the Caregiver. The Trustee can be an attorney, a financial institution, or anyone you trust. The Trustee should check in on your pet regularly to ensure they have a good quality of life. Ideally, the Trustee should be someone other than the person you designated as the Caregiver.

- **Caregiver:** Where will your pet live when you can no longer care for it yourself? You should choose someone who knows and loves your pet. What happens if you don't have anyone suitable? Ask your veterinarian, family members, and pet-sitters about becoming your pet's designated Caregiver or for any other ideas. You may also look online for pet-sitting services and begin testing out and interviewing potential Caregivers. Your Trust should provide reasonable compensation for the Caregiver and your pet's expenses.

- **Monitor:** A Monitor provides another set of eyes to ensure that the Caregiver and Trustee treat your pet well. Ideally, choose a Monitor that knows your pet and cares about animals. Your veterinarian may be an excellent choice for this role.

Tips for Creating a Pet Trust

You will need to work with an attorney to set up a Pet Trust. But here are some tips on what you need to take into consideration:

- When planning for your pet's future, assemble an information packet providing essential details, including your pet's medical history, needs, and preferences.

- You will also want to provide information about your wishes for end-of-life decision-making for your pet.

- You must determine how much money should go to the Pet Trust. It is important to consider the life expectancy of your pet, the number of pets you have, and the cost of caregiving and medical expenses.

- You must choose a "Remainder Beneficiary" to inherit any money left in the Trust upon your pet's death.

- If you don't have enough money to leave to a Pet Trust, consider purchasing a life insurance policy. You can designate your Pet Trust as the beneficiary of that policy.

I always enjoy talking with my clients about their pets and seeing their pictures. I have heard about some very smart and talented pets. I can tell how much they love them and the meaning and joy they bring to their lives. I know how important it is to them to ensure they will be cared for, even if something happens to them.

Common Questions About Supplemental Needs and Discretionary Trusts

Is a Supplemental Needs Trust the same as a Special Needs Trust?

The terms usually mean the same thing, but sometimes there is a difference in whether a friend or family member creates the Trust for the benefit of a disabled person or whether the disabled person establishes the Trust for their own benefit.

In what circumstances can a Supplemental Needs Trust be used?

The traditional Supplemental Needs Trust ensures that a person with disabilities can benefit from Trust assets without losing eligibility for government benefits. But it might be used for other vulnerable individuals and scenarios, for example:

- Elderly individuals who are incapacitated or require long term care.

- Individuals who are not classified as disabled but suffer from chronic illnesses or need extensive care.

What expenses can a Supplemental Needs Trust cover?

Supplemental Needs Trusts can cover a wide range of expenses such as education, health care not covered by Medicaid, recreational activities, travel, home modifications, personal care attendants, and other items or services that enhance the beneficiary's quality of life.

Can the beneficiary directly access the funds in the Trust?

The beneficiary cannot directly access the funds. A Trustee manages the Trust and makes disbursements on behalf of the beneficiary. True Link offers a credit card that the Trustee can establish for the beneficiary to use, providing limits and rules on spending. It is an excellent way to give the beneficiary independence safely.

Can a Supplemental Needs Trust be revoked or amended?

It depends on the type of Trust. A Third-Party Supplemental Needs Trust (one set up by someone other than the beneficiary) can typically be amended or revoked by the party who set it up (e.g., a parent or grandparent). A First-Party Supplemental Needs Trust (established by the beneficiary themselves) is usually irrevocable once established.

In what circumstances can a Discretionary Trust be used?

A Discretionary Trust can be used in any situation where you think it would be best for someone other than your intended beneficiary to manage and control the assets. It may be helpful in the following circumstances:

- If you want to spread out the inheritance you leave to your child
- If you are concerned about substance abuse
- If you are concerned about recklessness
- If you are concerned about a controlling spouse or partner or a risky marriage

The Trustee will decide when distributions should be made rather than the beneficiary.

What happens to the funds in the Trust after the beneficiary's death?

When a disabled person creates a Trust for their own benefit, the state usually requires a "pay back" provision at the end of their life. If any money remains in the Trust, it must be paid to the state to the extent it paid for their care.

Trusts created by a friend or a family member for the benefit of a disabled person do not typically require a "pay back" provision. These trusts can name a successor beneficiary, someone to receive any money remaining in the Trust.

Common Questions About Pet Trusts

What animals can be covered by a Pet Trust?

A Pet Trust can cover any pet, including dogs, cats, birds, horses, and exotic pets. The Trust can be tailored to meet the needs of your specific pet or multiple pets.

What expenses can a pet Trust cover?

A Pet Trust can cover many expenses, including food, veterinary care, grooming, boarding, and any special needs your pet may have. You can also include provisions for toys, treats, and other items to ensure your pet's quality of life.

Can I include specific instructions for my pet's care in the Pet Trust?

Yes, you can include detailed instructions on how your pet should be cared for, including feeding routines, medical care, exercise, and any other preferences you have for your pet's well-being.

How much money should I set aside in a Pet Trust?

The amount will depend on your pet's needs and expected lifespan. Consider ongoing expenses like food, veterinary care, and your pet's special requirements. Your veterinarian can help estimate costs.

What happens if the funds in the Pet Trust run out?

If the funds run out, the Caregiver may need to cover the remaining costs or find alternative arrangements for the pet's care.

What happens to the funds in the Trust if my pet passes away?

You can specify in the Trust document what happens to any remaining funds after your pet's death. Common options include donating to a charity, giving to a family member, or transferring the funds to your estate.

Can a Pet Trust be revoked or amended?

A Pet Trust can be either revocable or irrevocable. A Revocable Trust can be changed or canceled during your lifetime, while you cannot change an Irrevocable Trust once established.

Are Pet Trusts recognized in all states?

Most states recognize Pet Trusts, but the specific laws and requirements can vary. An attorney can provide guidance on the laws in your state.

Can I have a Pet Trust and a Will?

Yes, you should have both if you have a Pet Trust. A Will can address the disposition of your property and other matters, while a Pet Trust specifically addresses the care of your pet. If you only choose one document, it needs to be the Will. A Pet Trust is an extra. If you prefer to keep things simple in your Will, you can designate a Pet Caregiver and provide a stipend to that person to care for your pet.

• • • •

Taking care of your loved ones is an act of love and responsibility. Estate planning helps ensure they are provided for and protected according to your wishes. An attorney can help you create a plan tailored to your child's or pet's needs. It will make all the difference to those you care about and give you peace of mind.

7. GIFTING DURING YOUR LIFE

"For it is in giving that we receive."
—*Peace Prayer of St. Francis of Assisi*

Instead of waiting until you die to leave a meaningful legacy, this chapter focuses on gifting during your life. The following stories highlight how generosity can bring joy and companionship to you and those you love, allowing you to see the difference you are making.

Frank

One of my clients, Frank, wanted to make a gift to charity during his life. He had over $1 million and owned his home, so he felt confident he could meet his future needs.

Frank was a retired teacher and had always cared about children. After hearing about a Boys and Girls Club needing new computers for the children to do their homework, he reached out to learn more. Frank discovered the total cost for the project was $20,000 and donated the full amount. The club was extremely grateful, inviting Frank to visit and meet the kids. Afterward, Frank started volunteering at the club to help the kids with homework. Helping the children and getting to know the staff made him happy. His gift transformed the club and enriched his life, giving him a new purpose and fulfillment.

Lily

Lily generously shared experiences with her friends, nieces, and nephews. She was a passionate opera lover and held season tickets to the Met in New York City. Several times per year, she would invite a friend or relative to join her at the opera.

Many of her loved ones would not have had the opportunity to experience the opera without her generous invitations. Lily would cover all expenses for these special weekends in New York, staying in beautiful hotels and taking her guests out to fabulous dinners.

Lily loved creating cherished memories with those she cared about. She lived a vibrant life until the age of 96, traveling the world, cruising around the tip of Antarctica, and even going hot-air ballooning at 93. She often invited her friends on these wonderful trips and paid for their expenses. Rather than waiting to leave her assets to her loved ones after her death, Lily chose to share wonderful experiences with them during her lifetime.

Things to Consider Before Gifting

Generosity can enhance your life and the lives of others. However, before you start giving away money or other assets, it's important to understand the potential implications. There are three areas to consider before gifting. Let's look at these one by one:

Ensuring Your Own Needs Are Met

Before making a significant gift to any charity or person, please thoroughly consider whether this is a good idea, given your circumstances, especially your health and finances. You need to make sure you have enough money to maintain a comfortable quality of life, fulfill your financial commitments, and build a large safety net in case your expenses increase due to changes in health.

If you're uncertain about your ongoing expenses, a financial advisor can help create a projection that accounts for the ever-increasing cost of living.

Many individuals are shocked by the substantial costs associated with long term care. As health declines, the expenses for maintaining independence can far exceed expectations. It's not uncommon for individuals to expend $400,000 or more during their lifetime to pay for their care. Therefore, it's important to prioritize planning for these expenses before making any significant gifts, even if you don't think it will ever happen to you. Having the financial resources to cover your care gives you the freedom to choose your preferred form of care and helps you avoid being forced to go to a nursing home due to financial constraints. Please ensure that your current and future needs are met before making large gifts to others. Once you give the money away, you won't be able to get it back.

Impact on Public Benefits—Medicaid

Unless you have substantial assets and are unlikely to need public benefits, you must be thoughtful when making large gifts. If you run out of funds to pay for your care and need to rely on Medicaid benefits, the gifts you make may result in a significant problem.

When applying for Medicaid, you must disclose all gifts made within the five years preceding your application—commonly known as the "look-back period." If you made gifts during this time, they will impose a "penalty period," which delays your eligibility for Medicaid benefits. The penalty period is calculated based on the total gifts made during the look-back period. In Massachusetts, Medicaid closely scrutinizes gifts over $1,000.

If you have made gifts over this amount within the five years before applying for Medicaid and you later need Medicaid benefits, you may need to ask the recipient to return the money. There is no guarantee they will or can return it. Those with less than $1 million in assets should know the potential consequences gifting has on Medicaid eligibility. Gifting for any reason may cause problems if you (or your spouse) need nursing home care within the next five years. While small gifts for Christmas, birthdays, weddings, and graduations are unlikely to cause issues, more substantial gifts can trigger a penalty period. If you want to be more generous, it is better to space out your gifts over an extended period. For example, if you're going to gift $6,000 to your favorite charity, $500 per month over one year may be better than paying it all in one lump sum.

Paying the expenses for a few guests to join you on a vacation or experience is unlikely to cause a problem and will likely not be considered a gift.

Since it is not possible to know if you will need nursing home care within the next five years, please consider the following before making a gift:

- If your health is failing and your assets are under $800,000, check with an elder law attorney before making any gift over a few thousand dollars.

- If your spouse is ill and may need nursing home care, check with an elder law attorney before making substantial gifts.

- If you make a significant gift, do you have enough money to pay for five years of nursing home care? Nursing home care often costs $15,000 monthly or more, depending on where you live. Therefore, you will need approximately $900,000 in assets to ensure you can pay for your care for five years.

- There are exceptions to the five-year "look back" rule for gifts made to your spouse, a child who lived with you and took care of you, disabled persons, or a sibling who lives with you and has an equity interest in your home. You will need further guidance from an elder law attorney to take advantage of these exceptions.

Tax Implications

You need to consider several things when making significant gifts regarding taxes. These are:

- **Filing a Gift Tax Return**

  You must file a gift tax return if you make a gift over the annual limit the IRS sets (Note in 2025, the limit is $19,000 per person, per year). If you do, you must file a Form 709 with the IRS. However, you will likely not owe any tax. As of 2025, the IRS allows each person to gift up to $13.99 million during their lifetime before imposing a tax. You must file the return so the IRS can keep track of the amount given. No tax will be due if you haven't given away more than this during your lifetime. Most people don't need to worry much about the federal gift tax rules.

- **Tax Consequences of Gifting Appreciated Assets, Like Real Estate**

  When giving away an asset that has increased in value, it's important to consider the potential capital gains tax implications. Please consider the following about giving away appreciated assets:

  - Some appreciated assets may receive a "Step Up in Basis" upon your death. This means that, when determining whether capital gains tax is due, the IRS will use the asset's value at the time of your death rather than the actual amount you paid for the asset.

  - If you plan to give away any appreciated asset, check with an accountant or elder law attorney about the income tax consequences before making the gift. For assets that have appreciated significantly in value, it may be better to hold the asset until your death to avoid capital gains taxes or establish a Charitable Remainder Trust (more on this later in this chapter).

- Withdrawing money from a retirement account (unless it is a Roth IRA) has significant income tax consequences. I do not recommend withdrawing money from your retirement account to make a gift without consulting an accountant first. Otherwise, you could find yourself in trouble with the IRS.

- Giving a gift of an asset that has not gone up in value is usually preferred over giving away assets that have appreciated in value.

- **Impact of Gifting on Estate Tax**

  Gifting helps minimize the estate taxes due at the end of your life. Individuals or married couples with significant assets living in a state with a low estate tax threshold may want to consider ways to reduce their estate tax liability, including establishing trusts and annual gifting. Including charities in your estate can also help reduce estate taxes.

  Most Americans don't need to worry about paying federal estate taxes because, in 2025, the threshold is $13.99 million for individuals and $27.98 million for married couples. However, 17 states, plus the District of Columbia, currently have their own estate tax limits. Oregon has the worst estate tax law in the country, imposing an estate tax on estates over $1 million.

  Most solo seniors should not be too concerned about estate taxes unless they have significant assets. You won't ever pay the tax, but your estate will. If you are concerned about this, discuss your options with an estate planning or elder law attorney.

- **Inheritance Tax**

  Five states impose an inheritance tax on beneficiaries, regardless of the total size of the estate. These states are currently Kentucky, Maryland, Nebraska, New Jersey, and Pennsylvania.

Unlike estate taxes, which are paid by the estate before distributions are made, inheritance taxes are paid by the recipient. The tax rate depends on the beneficiary's relationship to the deceased—spouses, children, and grandchildren are often exempt or taxed at lower rates, while more distant relatives or non-family members may face higher taxes.

If you live in one of these five states and have significant assets that you want to leave to someone who is not exempt from the inheritance tax in your state, you may want to meet with a local elder law attorney to discuss a gifting strategy. Gifts made during your lifetime generally avoid inheritance tax.

- **Donor Advised Funds**

A Donor-Advised Fund (DAF) is a simple way to give to charity while enjoying immediate tax benefits. It allows you to contribute assets—such as cash, stocks, or real estate—into a dedicated charitable account, take an upfront tax deduction, and decide over time which charities will receive grants.

For example, Julia sold her home for a significant profit, which would be subject to income tax. She wanted to donate some of her proceeds to charity. She wasn't sure which organizations she wanted to support long-term, but she knew this was a high-income year, and a charitable deduction would be helpful. Instead of making one large donation, she opened a Donor Advised Fund through Vanguard. By contributing $50,000 to her DAF, she received an immediate tax deduction. Over the following years, Julia used the fund to support various causes she cared about, including local food banks and environmental nonprofits. She liked that she did not need to decide everything at once.

A DAF also simplifies record-keeping—Julia no longer had to keep track of multiple donation receipts, as all her giving was managed through one account. When she updated her estate plan, she arranged for the remaining balance in her DAF to be donated to a scholarship fund in her name, ensuring her legacy would continue beyond her lifetime.

A DAF is a powerful way to support causes over time, simplify charitable giving, and leave a lasting impact—all while gaining potential tax advantages.

Charitable Remainder Trusts

A Charitable Remainder Trust may make sense if you have a lot of money and want to provide for yourself or other beneficiaries while leaving a significant gift to charity. It is particularly advantageous if you own highly appreciated assets and want to avoid large capital gains taxes.

> *A Charitable Remainder Trust is an Irrevocable Trust that provides an income stream to you or other designated beneficiaries for a specified period, with the remainder of the assets going to a designated charity at the end of the Trust term.*

In addition to the charitable impact, the Charitable Remainder Trust has two significant benefits: potential tax deductions and income stream.

The process of creating a Charitable Remainder Trust is as follows:

- You must create the Charitable Remainder Trust and change your assets' title into the Trust's name.

- The Trust will then pay out a part of the income from the assets within it to you or other Beneficiaries for a specific period or even for the rest of your life.

- Once this period ends, the Trustee pays the remaining assets in the Trust to the charity of your choice.

One of the great things about the Charitable Remainder Trust is that you may receive a tax deduction based on the estimated remainder that will eventually go to the charity. Plus, the assets in the Trust are excluded from your estate, which could help reduce estate taxes.

A Charitable Remainder Trust can be a great solution if you want to support a charity while also receiving income from your assets during your lifetime. If you want to create a Charitable Remainder Trust, consult an attorney.

Common Questions About Gifting

What is considered a gift in legal terms?

In legal terms, a gift is a voluntary transfer of property (such as money, real estate, or personal items) from one person to another without expecting anything in return.

Can I gift assets other than cash?

You can give various types of assets, including stocks, bonds, real estate, and personal property.

Is there a limit to how much I can gift without paying taxes?

The annual gift tax exclusion is $19,000 per recipient (in 2025). This means you can gift up to $19,000 to any individual in a year without filing a gift tax return or paying any gift taxes.

Please never cash in deferred tax retirement benefits to give a gift. You must pay ordinary income tax when withdrawing money from a retirement account.

What if I want to give more than the annual exclusion amount?

You must file a gift tax return if you give more than $19,000 per recipient in one year. However, you will not necessarily owe taxes because you can apply the gift against your lifetime estate and gift tax exemption, which is $13.99 million in 2025.

What is "gift splitting," and how does it work?

Gift splitting allows a married couple to combine their gift tax exclusions, doubling the amount they can give to a single recipient without triggering gift taxes. For example, in 2025, a couple could jointly give $38,000 to an individual without needing to file a gift tax return.

Will the recipient of the gift owe tax?

Generally, when you give a gift to someone, they do not owe any tax on that gift, regardless of the amount.

Can I make a gift to my spouse without any tax implications?

You can make unlimited gifts to your spouse without any tax implications, provided your spouse is a U.S. citizen. If your spouse is not a U.S. citizen, there is an annual exclusion limit of $190,000 in 2025.

Are there any types of gifts that are not subject to gift taxes?

Gifts that are not currently subject to gift taxes include:

- Unlimited gifts to spouses if the spouse is a U.S. citizen.

- Tuition payments paid directly to an educational institution for someone else's education.

- Medical expenses paid directly to a medical provider for someone else's medical care.

- Qualified charitable donations are not subject to gift taxes.

How can I set up a Donor Advised Fund?

A Donor Advised Fund (DAF) is set up through a sponsoring organization such as Fidelity Charitable, Schwab Charitable, Vanguard Charitable, or a community foundation. Many financial advisors can guide you through the process.

Can I get back the money I contributed to a donor-advised fund?

No. Once you contribute to a Donor Advised Fund (DAF), the funds are irrevocable and must be used for charitable purposes. While you retain control over recommending grants to charities and investment decisions, you cannot withdraw the money for personal use.

Which is easier to set up: a Donor Advised Fund or a Charitable Remainder Trust?

A Donor Advised Fund is much easier and faster to set up than a Charitable Remainder Trust (CRT). A DAF can be opened in minutes with a financial institution or community foundation, requires minimal paperwork, and has no legal fees. A CRT, on the other hand, requires an attorney, formal trust documents, ongoing administration, and higher setup costs. If you're looking for a simple way to give to charity, a DAF is the easier option.

Compared to a Donor Advised Fund, what is the biggest benefit of a Charitable Remainder Trust?

The biggest benefit of a Charitable Remainder Trust (CRT) is that it provides an income stream for life or a set period of time while still allowing you to leave money to charity. Unlike a Donor Advised Fund, which does not pay anything back to the donor, a CRT lets you receive income from the trust assets before the remaining funds go to charity. This makes it a good option for those who want to support a cause but still need income from their assets.

• • • •

Giving can bring great joy to you and those you care about. However, balancing generosity with ensuring your needs are met is crucial. Before making significant gifts, you need to understand the tax implications and how gifting might affect your eligibility for public benefits. Consulting with a financial advisor or attorney can provide valuable guidance.

8. PREPARING FOR AN EMERGENCY

"By failing to prepare, you are preparing to fail."
—Benjamin Franklin

How will the people you rely on in an emergency know you need them?

The consequences can be devastating when solo seniors don't have a reliable emergency response system. Over the years, I have been appointed by the court to serve as a Guardian for individuals who had no one to step in when they needed help. Unfortunately, many of these situations were discovered after days of waiting.

One such case involved Donna, who had fallen by her back door and screamed for help for two days before a neighbor finally heard her and called 911. When the firefighters arrived, they found her in critical condition. Another case was Victor, who attended a local senior center regularly. When he failed to show up for several days, the center's staff called for a wellness check. He was found lying on the floor, unable to get up. In the most tragic cases, I've been appointed as a Public Administrator when no one found the person until it was too late, their bodies decomposing inside their homes.

These are heartbreaking examples of what can happen to those who do not have an emergency plan. While ensuring you have legal documents is essential, having a reliable emergency response plan is just as crucial. This chapter will walk you through building a system that works for you so your trusted individuals are notified when you need them most.

Setting Up an Emergency Contact System

An effective emergency system in place involves a few components and steps. Let's look at them one by one, starting with the basics.

Step 1: Create "In Case of Emergency" Card

An "In Case of Emergency" (ICE) card is a small, portable card that contains vital personal information. It is meant to help first responders, medical personnel, or bystanders identify you and call your designated contacts if you need urgent assistance.

An ICE card typically looks like a credit card or driver's license. The front often features a prominent "In Case of Emergency" label.

The card should include essential information that first responders need to manage your care and quickly notify the right people. You need to include:

- Your full name
- The names and phone numbers of your first and second Health Care Proxies or your most relied-upon contact
- Key medical conditions (e.g., diabetes, heart condition, allergies)
- Essential medications (if space permits)
- If you have a DNR/DNI order, include this on the card (e.g., "DNR in effect")
- If you have a pet, include this on the card.

You can create an ICE card at home by downloading a template. If possible, laminate the card to protect it from wear and tear. You can also buy blank emergency cards from Amazon, medical supply stores, pharmacies, and specialty websites. A Medical Alert Card typically ranges from $5 to $20.

Medical Alert Bracelet

In addition to an ICE card, you can have a Medical Alert Bracelet. This wearable accessory provides critical medical information. It is typically made of stainless steel and has an engraved plate or tag with essential details.

The information on the bracelet usually includes:

- Your medical conditions (e.g., diabetes, epilepsy, allergies)
- Medications or treatments (e.g., insulin-dependent, blood thinner)
- Emergency contact numbers
- Any other relevant medical instructions (e.g., "No MRI," "Pacemaker")
- Some bracelets also have a QR code or a phone number that links to an online profile for more detailed medical information.

A medical Alert Bracelet costs between $20 and $100 and can be purchased from online retailers, medical supply stores, pharmacies, specialty websites, jewelry stores, print services, or health care providers.

Step 2: Use a Medical Alert System

If you live alone and are at risk of falling or have a medical condition, consider investing in a medical alert system like Lifeline or Medical Guardian. A Medical Alert System typically includes a wearable device with a button you can push in an emergency that connects you to a 24/7 monitoring center. Key features may include two-way communication, automatic fall detection, and GPS tracking.

The typical cost for a basic plan, which usually includes 24/7 monitoring and an emergency button, ranges from $20 to $60 per month. Systems with additional features, like automatic fall detection, GPS tracking, or mobile capabilities, can cost more. Some insurance plans or programs cover part of the expense.

Step 3: Use A Daily Check-In Service

Services like "I Am Fine" offer daily check-in calls to ensure that solo seniors are safe. There are likely to be alternative apps on your phone, as well. This is how it works:

- You receive a daily automated phone call asking you to confirm that you are fine by pressing 1.
- If you don't respond, the service will call you four more times within the hour.
- If there is still no response, the service will alert your designated emergency contact to check in on you.

This provides an affordable layer of safety, particularly if you plan to age in place. It ensures that someone will be notified if you cannot respond and offers peace of mind.

Step 4: Share Your Health Care Proxy with Your Doctor

Ensure that your doctor has copies of your Health Care Proxy in your medical records. By doing this, any medical professional who treats you will know whom to contact if you cannot make decisions for yourself.

Step 5: Inform a Trusted Neighbor or Friend

I recommend sharing basic emergency information with a nearby friend or neighbor. Often, a neighbor is the first person to realize that there is a problem. Make sure they know how to contact your Health Care Proxy in an emergency.

Step 6: Regularly Update Your Emergency Plan

Life circumstances and contacts change, so reviewing and updating your emergency plan is important. Check that all emergency contacts are current and that your Health Care Proxy and Power of Attorney have access to the latest copies of your legal documents. Also, ensure your doctor, medical alert system, and neighbors have the correct information to ensure smooth communication during an emergency.

Having an updated emergency plan can make the difference between having your wishes honored and losing control. Martha's story provides an example of a solid emergency plan that worked when she needed it.

Martha

Martha lived alone in a small apartment in Boston. She had a niece, Emily, who lived a few hours away and whom she had appointed as her Health Care Proxy. Martha took steps to prepare for an emergency, such as listing her niece as the Emergency contact on her phone, giving her primary care doctor copies of her Health Care Proxy document, making sure Emily had copies of all important legal documents, and giving her neighbor a copy of her emergency contact card. Martha also wore a medical alert bracelet from Lifeline.

One afternoon, Martha experienced dizziness and collapsed in her kitchen. The Lifeline system detected the fall and immediately dispatched emergency services. She listed her niece as a contact in the Lifeline system. Lifeline contacted the niece to let her know there was an emergency. Martha's neighbor noticed the ambulance arrive and provided the paramedics with her emergency contact card details.

The paramedics quickly transported Martha to the hospital. Since her doctor had already uploaded her Health Care Proxy, the hospital contacted Emily. Within hours, her niece spoke to the doctors and made important decisions on Martha's behalf.

Thanks to Martha's careful planning, all the pieces fell into place quickly. Her emergency response system worked seamlessly, and the people she needed were there.

• • • •

Take the time to set up your emergency response system now. In an emergency, every minute counts, and ensuring the right people are notified can make all the difference. To get started, you can complete the vital information at the end of this book or visit www.SoloAllies.com to download your free Solo Senior Organizer, which includes important emergency information for you to complete.

PART II:
PLANNING
FOR A SECURE
FINANCIAL FUTURE

PART II:
PLANNING
FOR A SECURE
FINANCIAL FUTURE

9. PREPARING
FOR YOUR FINANCIAL FUTURE

*"The first step towards getting somewhere is to decide that
you are not going to stay where you are."*

—*J.P. Morgan*

In Part I of this book, we covered the essential legal documents that provide a safety net in case of emergencies and make your wishes known and honored. Now, in Part II, we focus on planning for financial security.

I am not a financial expert. However, in working with clients for over 25 years, as an elder law attorney, I have seen the good, bad, and the ugly, when it comes to being financially prepared for the future. I have a few tips to help you avoid some of the mistakes I have seen.

Whether you feel overwhelmed by managing money or are confident in handling your finances, we will explore four key areas: assessing your current situation, setting goals, budgeting, making good decisions, understanding investments to avoid, and being aware of scams. Let's look at them one by one.

Assessing Your Current Financial Situation

Even if you decide to seek help from a financial advisor, you'll need to provide them with information about your current situation. Get organized by taking the following steps:

- **Calculate your net worth:** List all your assets, like savings, investments, and property, and add their current values. From that number, subtract your liabilities, like mortgage, credit card debt, loans, etc. The number you end up with is your current net worth.

- **Track your income:** List all your income sources, such as income from working, Social Security, or pensions, dividends, investments or rents you collect. Calculate your monthly and annual revenue.

- **Track your expenses:** List all your expenses, such as your mortgage, rent, insurance, health care, household, etc. Calculate your monthly and annual expenses.

This exercise provides a picture of where you are now.

Setting Financial Goals

Setting clear financial goals helps you focus on what truly matters to you. How do you envision your future? Some goals might be about having peace of mind, enjoying yourself, ensuring a high quality of life, leaving a legacy, and making a difference in the lives of others.

Here are some examples of goals:

- Establishing an emergency fund
- Planning for long term care costs
- Paying off your debts
- Having enough money to travel
- Saving enough money to live in a supportive community
- Not having to worry about money
- Being generous with others

You need to prioritize your goals based on their urgency, importance, and your specific circumstances. Make sure to differentiate between needs and wants and to set realistic deadlines for achieving these goals. You can create two lists: one for short-term objectives within the next six months or year and another for long term goals over the next five years or more.

Finding the Right Balance
Between Enjoying Life and Saving

While planning for your financial future and potential long-term care needs is important, it is important to strike a balance and enjoy life while you can. I have worked with clients who were so focused on saving for the future that they denied themselves even the simplest joys—never going on vacation, avoiding dining out, or refusing to buy things that would have improved their daily lives.

Being financially responsible doesn't mean depriving yourself of a fulfilling life. Yes, setting aside an emergency fund and planning for potential care costs is wise, but life is happening now. If you are physically able to do so and you can afford it, take that trip, go to the concert, treat yourself to a good meal, or spend money on hobbies and experiences that bring you joy.

If the time comes when you need long-term care and your funds run out, Medicaid will pay for your care. The options may be more limited, but you will not be left without help. Finding the right balance—one that gives you peace of mind about the future while allowing you to enjoy the present—is the key to financial well-being.

Creating a Plan

Once you do the hard work of assessing your current financial situation and thinking about your goals, the next step is to figure out how to get there. You may already be on the right track. However, if your costs are high or your income is limited, something needs to change. There are strategies to help you reach your goals.

One strategy to save money is to cut your expenses. Small changes can result in significant savings over time. For example, if you are eating out frequently, try cooking at home more often. If you love to shop, be mindful and only buy what you need. Take a look at your monthly subscriptions and bills. You may find that you are paying for services you never use or that you can switch to a more affordable option, such as a cheaper cell phone or cable package. Making bigger changes, like moving to a less expensive home or driving a less expensive car, can have an even greater impact.

If reducing expenses is not enough to balance your budget, consider ways to increase your income. A part-time job could provide additional money. Many flexible work-from-home opportunities are available today, which could be a good fit. There is a wonderful company called Seniors Helping Seniors, www.seniorshelpingseniors.com, which hires seniors to provide companionship and assistance to seniors who need support to live independently. This can be a great way to make money and connect with others.

Managing Savings, Pensions, and Benefits

As a solo senior, having a solid retirement savings plan is crucial. Hopefully, you have a pension plan or contributed to an IRA or 401K. If you have, there are certain things to consider:

- **Traditional IRA or 401K:** The withdrawals are taxed as ordinary income. This means that even with substantial savings, taxes can significantly reduce the amount you receive when you withdraw money. Depending upon your income tax bracket, you will need to withhold 20%-38% when withdrawing this money. Also, remember that once you reach age 72, you must withdraw a minimum amount from certain retirement accounts each year to avoid penalties with the IRS.

- **Work Pension:** Many retirees have pensions from their employers that offer the option of a lump sum payment or a monthly guaranteed amount, often called an annuity. Here are four things to consider when deciding what option to take:

- The lump sum payment option allows you to use your money as you see fit. You can invest it, use it to pay off debts or spend it as needed. You may achieve higher returns than if you annuitized it. However, this option requires discipline. If you struggle to control your spending or make wise investment decisions, this might not be your best choice.

- An annuity provides a steady, predictable income for a specific term or the rest of your life. However, once you choose an annuity, you usually can't change your mind or access a large sum for unexpected expenses. Unless your annuity is indexed for inflation, your income could lose purchasing power over time.

- In some situations, a lower income might be better, especially if you ever need to rely on public benefit programs or subsidized senior housing. Although you may have plenty of money right now, long term care costs are very expensive and you may need to rely on these programs in the future. If you are concerned about this, a lump sum payment may be the better choice. If you are confused or think you need to rely upon public benefit programs in the future, consult with an elder law attorney or financial advisor.

- Life expectancy is a factor. Many annuities only make payments during your life. Others may provide a guaranteed minimum time that the annuity will make payments, even if you die within that time. It is important to understand the agreement and consider your life expectancy. If you are sick or do not think that you will live a long a long life, the lump sum payment is likely the better option. When in doubt seek guidance.

Social Security Retirement Benefits

You must decide when to start receiving your Social Security Retirement Benefits. The timing can significantly impact the amount you receive. The Social Security Administration allows you to receive Retirement Benefits as early as age 62. However, taking benefits early will reduce your monthly payments compared to what you would receive if you wait until your Full Retirement Age (FRA). This option might make sense if you need more income at age 62 or your life expectancy is short.

Your Full Retirement Age is when you become eligible to receive your full Social Security Retirement Benefits. The exact age depends on your birth year, typically between 66 and 67. Alternatively, you can delay taking Social Security Retirement Benefits beyond your FRA to receive a higher monthly payment. For each year you wait, up to age 70, your benefit amount will increase.

Deciding when to take Social Security Retirement Benefits can be complicated and depends on your circumstances. If you are not sure what to do, consult a financial advisor. If you may need to rely on public benefit programs like Medicaid for future care, you should speak with an elder law attorney. They can help you understand your options for protecting your assets and help determine if your income needs to be under a certain amount to qualify for Medicaid benefits.

In some cases, it may be better to take your Social Security Retirement Benefits sooner to avoid exceeding Medicaid's income limit in the future. This significant decision can impact your financial security and quality of life as you age.

Financial Advisors

A financial advisor helps clients manage their finances by focusing on budgeting, investment strategies, retirement planning, tax strategies, and risk management. While financial advisors can be helpful, they are not always needed. Whether you should hire one depends on your unique situation. Here, I will review the pros and cons of hiring a financial advisor, what to consider when selecting one, and their role in securing your financial future.

- **The Pros:** Having a good financial advisor can help. They are experts at managing money, investing savings, and lowering taxes. With their knowledge and experience, they can guide you in making wise decisions and avoiding costly mistakes. You can create a solid financial plan, make smart investments, and even increase your savings over time. Plus, when a trustworthy professional handles your finances, you will have less stress, giving you more time to enjoy your life.

- **The Cons:** While hiring a financial advisor can offer many benefits, it's also important to consider the downsides. One of the main cons is the cost. Advisors can be expensive, and their fees can cut into your investment returns over time.

Another risk is that Advisors, especially those who earn commissions from selling financial products, may be motivated to recommend products that make them higher commissions, even if those aren't the best fit for you.

Unfortunately, there is also the risk of fraud. Look for a financial advisor who is considered a "fiduciary." This means they must always act in their client's best interest, prioritizing their needs above their own. The term fiduciary in this context does not mean they will act as your Power of Attorney, Health Care Proxy, or Executor.

Tips for Working With a Financial Advisor

Here are some tips to help you make the most of your relationship with your financial advisor and protect yourself:

- Your financial advisor should never serve as your Power of Attorney.

- For most seniors, the financial advisor should only make diversified, low-risk investments and help you make your money last for the rest of your life.

- Consider inviting a knowledgeable friend or attorney to meet with you and your financial advisor to ensure the recommended investments are in your best interest.

Do-It-Yourself Money Management Tips

If you prefer to manage your own finances. Here are some tips that you might find helpful:

- Consider low-risk investments like Bank CDs, bonds, or money market accounts.

- Sometimes, purchasing several Bank CDs with varying terms can be a good, low-risk way to diversify your investments.

- It is important to consider the Federal Deposit Insurance Corporation (FDIC) insurance limits. The FDIC is an agency of the United States government that insures deposits up to $250,000 per depositor, per insured bank, for each account ownership category. If your total deposits at one bank exceed this limit, consider moving some funds to a different bank to ensure they are fully FDIC-insured.

- Vanguard has low-fee, do-it-yourself investment funds that are low-risk. They may offer some financial guidance as well.

Annuities

Financial advisors are often motivated to sell annuities because they receive a commission. I have seen many clients like Jack, who should have never bought an annuity.

Jack

Jack, an 82-year-old man, purchased an annuity for $350,000, which his financial advisor recommended. He received $3,200 monthly for the rest of his life in exchange for a lump sum. Combined with his monthly Social Security income of $1,800, he had just enough to pay for his modest needs. Within two years of purchasing the annuity, his health began to fail, and he needed home health aides for a few hours each day to continue living in his home safely. The monthly cost of a private home health aide was $5,000. He could not afford this, as he would not have any money to pay his rent, food, or essential expenses.

Jack met with me to determine if he could qualify for Medicaid benefits. I had to give Jack bad news. The annuity had put his income over the limit to qualify for Medicaid benefits. These benefits would have provided up to 40 hours of home health care per week. If he could cash in the annuity, then there would be a way for me to guide him. However, there was no way to cancel the annuity and get the remaining funds back.

If Jack had the $350,000, he would have been over the $2,000 asset limit and could not qualify for Medicaid benefits at home or in a nursing home. However, I could have guided him in spending this excess money in a way that would still benefit him, such as paying off his debts, renovating his home to be more accessible, and establishing a Pooled Disability Trust, which could be used to help meet his needs.

My client was forced to go to a nursing home when there could have been a way to keep him home if he had not purchased the annuity. Even worse, Jack could only keep $72.80 per month from his income. Even if you qualify for Medicaid benefits, you must still pay almost all your income to the nursing home each month. The financial advisor should have never recommended the annuity to an 82-year-old man, who would likely need to rely on Medicaid benefits to help pay for his care.

Things to Consider Before Purchasing an Annuity

I am generally wary of annuities, and seniors should be extra cautious before buying one. I recommend avoiding annuities unless you have more than enough money to cover your care costs and don't anticipate relying on public benefits.

In certain situations, particularly involving married couples, if one spouse requires nursing home care, an elder law attorney may suggest that the spouse still living at home buy an Immediate Annuity. Also known as a "Single-Premium Immediate Annuity" (SPIA), insurance companies provide these to offer a guaranteed income stream that begins after you pay a lump-sum payment. Nevertheless, these are typically not purchased until the spouse needs nursing home care, and they must fulfill specific criteria. It is important to purchase them with the careful guidance of an elder law attorney, who will consult with a financial advisor to ensure the annuity meets these criteria. If your financial advisor suggests purchasing an annuity, I recommend consulting an elder law attorney before making any decision.

Life Insurance

If you have a disabled child and limited assets, you might consider purchasing a life insurance policy. Otherwise, I would not recommend it. In my opinion, life insurance policies are not worth it or even necessary for most solo seniors. These policies do not have very good returns, and they are often hard to keep track of. I am sure many policies go uncashed after someone dies because no one knew they existed.

It also takes at least a few weeks after death to access the funds. If the funds are set aside to pay for funeral expenses, your funeral will likely have happened weeks before anyone will get the money from the policy. If you want to pay for your funeral, it is best to prepay it or ask an elder law attorney to help you set up a simple Funeral Trust. The main goal of a Funeral Trust is to cover the cost of things like the ceremony, casket, burial plot, cremation, and other related expenses.

If you already have a life insurance policy, be sure that your Attorney or the Executor/Personal Representative of your estate knows about the policy and has a copy. If no one knows about the policy, it will be useless.

Protecting Yourself from Scams

Scammers are everywhere. Unfortunately, you should assume every phone call, email, or letter is likely a scam. Even worse, there are people out there looking to prey on older adults. It is awful that we live in a world where we must be suspicious of everyone. For solo seniors, staying vigilant is essential to safeguard your financial and personal security.

One example is Bob, a man in his seventies with early dementia who fell victim to a ruthless contractor. Bob needed some repairs done on his home. He fell victim to a contractor who charged him outrageous amounts of money, totaling over $2 million for a small amount of work provided. The contractor would send a work crew into Bob's house to paint the same room over and over again and charge him $100,000 each time. When Bob's wife died, a family friend stepped in as Power of Attorney and realized something was wrong. She helped Bob bring a criminal action against the contractor.

Some scams seem obvious, but many are harder to detect.

Common Scams

Scammers use various methods to target seniors, from email phishing and fake tech support to emotional manipulation like grandparent or romance scams. Always be wary of unsolicited calls, emails, or offers that seem too good to be true. Legitimate organizations will never pressure you for immediate payment or ask for personal information over the phone or via email.

Tips to Stay Safe from Scams

- **Screen Your Calls:** Let unknown numbers go to voicemail. Scammers often rely on getting you on the phone.

- **Verify Before You Act:** If someone claims to represent a company or agency, contact them using a trusted source by hanging up and looking up the official contact information for the company they claim to be calling from, not the number or email they provide.

- **Protect Your Information:** Avoid sharing personal or financial details.

- **Be Skeptical of Pressure:** Scammers create urgency to manipulate decisions. Take time to verify facts before acting.

- **Monitor Your Accounts:** Regularly check bank and credit card statements for suspicious activity.

If you suspect fraud, report it to your local police. Being proactive and informed is your best defense. By staying cautious, you can protect yourself from scammers and preserve your financial and personal well-being. If something doesn't feel right, trust your instincts and seek advice from a friend, attorney, or financial advisor before proceeding.

Common Questions
About Preparing Your Finances

Can I rely on Social Security Retirement Benefits alone for retirement?

Social Security Retirement Benefits provides a steady income, but it is often insufficient to cover all of your living expenses. It's important to have additional sources of income, such as savings, investments, or government assistance programs.

Can I work while receiving Social Security Retirement Benefits?

You can work while receiving Social Security Retirement Benefits, but if you are below your Full Retirement Age (FRA), your benefits may be temporarily reduced if your earnings exceed certain limits.

What is the best age to start Social Security Retirement Benefits?

You can start receiving benefits as early as 62, but waiting until full retirement age (67) or delaying until age 70 can increase your monthly benefits. Delaying may be beneficial if you're concerned about long term financial security and don't need the money to meet your basic needs.

What are catch-up contributions?

If you are 50 or older, you can make additional contributions to your retirement accounts to accelerate savings as retirement nears. You can contribute to a 401K and an IRA, but annual contribution limits exist.

What is the difference between a Traditional IRA and a Roth IRA?

Traditional IRA contributions are tax-deductible because you pay taxes when you withdraw the money. Roth IRA contributions use after-tax dollars, and withdrawals during retirement are tax-free.

What are Required Minimum Distributions (RMDs), and how do they affect me?

Once you turn 73, you must start withdrawing a minimum amount from most retirement accounts like a 401K or Traditional IRA. Planning for these withdrawals is crucial because they are taxed at your regular income tax rate, and missing the deadline could result in penalties.

What are the tax consequences of withdrawing money from a 401K, Traditional IRA, or tax-deferred retirement account?

When you withdraw money from a tax-deferred retirement account, that income will be taxed at your ordinary income tax rate. It is important to remember this whenever you make withdrawals. If you need money and have nontax deferred assets, take the money you need from that asset or account first.

However, if you know that you will have significant medical expenses and need money to pay for those expenses, the income tax may be offset by the medical expense deduction. It is always a good idea to ask an accountant any questions.

How do Financial Advisors get paid?

Financial advisors get paid in several ways. Here are some common fee structures:

- **Hourly:** a good option if you only need a financial plan.

- **Flat fee:** a good option if you know what services you need.

- **Asset-based fee:** the advisor receives a percentage of the assets they manage.

- **Performance-based fee:** the advisor earns a fee based on the success of the investments.

- **Commission:** the advisor earns commissions from selling financial products.

Understanding how the advisor gets paid will help determine whether the financial advisor is looking out for your best interest or their own. A good financial advisor will always be transparent about how they get paid.

How do I find a Financial Advisor?

Looking for a financial advisor is like trying to find a trustworthy friend. You want someone who listens, understands your needs, and has your best interest at heart. You could start by asking your friends or attorney for recommendations or check out groups like the Financial Planning Association or the National Association of Personal Financial advisors to find certified pros in your area.

When you meet with a potential financial advisor, ask about their experience, approach to financial planning, and how they get paid. Shop around until you find someone you are comfortable with. The Securities and Exchange Commission provides a free website, www.sec.gov/litigations/sec-action-look-up, where you can see if the advisor you are considering has any complaints against them. Visit www.soloallies.com to find financial advisors who are senior certified.

• • • •

It is easy to get overwhelmed when planning for your financial future. However, this is a journey to take one step at a time. By assessing your current finances, thinking about your goals, creating a budget, understanding your options, being aware of safe investments, and avoiding scams, you will be on your way to taking control. There are resources and professionals ready to help you enjoy your future with peace of mind and financial stability!

10. PLANNING FOR HEALTH CARE AND LONG-TERM CARE COSTS

"Save your money. You're going to need twice as much in your old age as you think." — Michael Caine

Whether you are just starting to think about your future care needs or already considering your options, this chapter will help you navigate the maze of health care and long term options, like home care, assisted living, and nursing home care. Let's start by understanding the cost of long term care before we move on to how you can pay for it.

The Cost of Long-Term Care

No one knows what the future holds or what their care will cost. However, I can provide some estimates based on current costs in different settings. In Massachusetts, nursing home care typically exceeds $180,000 or more annually. Assisted living care can range from $80,000 to $150,000 per year. Private home care is often the most expensive option. If you only need a few hours of help per week, you can expect to pay around $40 per hour or more.

Statistics show that approximately 52% of those over 65 will need nursing home care at some point. The average length of stay in a nursing home is typically around two years. So, based on the above numbers, in Massachusetts, you have a 52% chance of spending $360,000 or more for nursing home care.

These costs can vary significantly in other parts of the country. I hope they are more reasonable in your area. While these numbers may scare you, there are resources and strategies to help you.

If you own real estate and have a few hundred thousand dollars or more in savings, you likely have enough money to pay for your long term care needs. However, suppose you don't have substantial savings or own your home. In that case, it is important to consider other options, such as long term care insurance or public benefit programs.

Long-Term Care Insurance

Long term care insurance allows you to receive assistance in different settings, such as at home, an assisted living facility, or a nursing home. However, whether you should purchase long term care insurance depends on your current health status and financial situation. If you are sick or diagnosed with a serious illness, finding a company willing to sell long term care insurance to you may be impossible. If you have a family history of dementia or Alzheimer's, it may be more important for you to buy long term care insurance.

Long term care insurance is expensive. The cost depends on the age when you purchase the policy, your gender (usually, women pay more), the benefit period, and the level of benefits, among other things. If paying the premiums will make it difficult to afford your basic needs and reach your personal goals, then you should not buy it. For example, if you won't be able to go out for dinner a few times per month or on a vacation once or twice per year, then I would recommend that you skip it. Enjoying life while you can is important, too.

If you have enough money to pay for whatever care you need and still have money left over at the end of your life, a long term care insurance policy may not be worth it. If this is the case, it depends on how important it is for you to leave money to others at the end of your life, even if you need expensive long term care.

Long term care insurance is one way to plan for your future. However, it doesn't make sense for everyone. If you cannot afford long term care insurance and you run out of money, Medicaid will pay for your care in a nursing home.

Government Benefit Programs

There are several public programs that help pay for health care and long term care. These are Medicare, Medicaid, PACE, and veterans' programs. Let's look at what they cover.

Medicare

Medicare is a federal program available to most seniors over 65, regardless of how much money they have. Medicare is divided into two parts, each covering specific services.

- **Medicare Part A** covers hospital stays, limited short-term nursing home care, and home health care coverage. Under Part A, if you have a hospital stay of at least three nights, Medicare can cover a short-term stay in a skilled nursing facility for up to 100 days. However, most people don't receive the full 100 days of coverage because you must be making progress toward your rehabilitation to qualify. A co-pay is required after the first 20 days, unless you have supplemental insurance. When Medicare coverage ends, if you still need to stay in the nursing home, you will pay for your care. In Massachusetts, this can cost around $500 per day. If you can't afford this, you may be eligible to apply for Medicaid.

- **Medicare Part B** covers doctor's visits, outpatient care, medical supplies, and preventive services. Medicare Part B provides very limited home care services, usually only after leaving the hospital.

While Medicare provides some coverage for care, it is limited and typically short-term. You can't rely on it to cover long term home care. Understanding this can help you plan for the costs you incur and explore other options.

Medicare Advantage Plans

Medicare Advantage Plans, offered by private insurers, are an alternative to the federal government's Original Medicare (Parts A and B). These plans often include benefits like drug coverage (Part D) and extra services like dental or vision, all in the same plan. I recommend avoiding Medicare Advantage Plans because they have significant downsides:

- **Limited Provider Networks:** These plans typically restrict access to a narrow network of doctors and hospitals, which can be a problem for seniors needing specialized care or living in areas with fewer health care options.

- **Fewer Accepted Facilities:** Some skilled nursing facilities, rehabilitation centers, and hospitals don't accept Medicare Advantage due to lower reimbursement rates. This limits your care options.

- **Prior Authorization Requirements:** Many plans require approval before treatments, tests, or hospital stays, creating delays and hassles.

- **Shorter Rehabilitation Coverage:** Medicare Advantage often limits the number of days covered for rehabilitation after a hospital stay, forcing seniors to leave sooner or pay privately, unlike Original Medicare, which tends to offer more coverage.

- **Difficulties Switching Back to Original Medicare:** Returning to Original Medicare is only allowed during the annual "Open Enrollment Period" (Oct 15–Dec 7). Switching outside this may be impossible, and exceptions vary by state.

While Medicare Advantage Plans may appear more cost-effective upfront, especially for those without medical care, they can cost you more in the long run. Original Medicare, combined with a Medigap policy, often offers far more flexibility and security, especially if your health care needs increase.

Medigap Policies

Medigap policies, or Medicare Supplement Insurance, are private insurance plans that cover out-of-pocket costs like copayments and deductibles not covered by Original Medicare. These standardized plans offer the same benefits across all insurers. Available only to those with Original Medicare, they don't cover dental, vision, or long term care services. However, they provide more flexibility in choosing doctors and hospitals.

Medicaid

Medicaid differs from Medicare because it only helps people who meet certain financial criteria. Qualifying requires an application process and proof of limited assets or income. Medicaid helps seniors stay at home or pay for nursing home care.

- **Assisted Living Facilities:** Sometimes, Medicaid programs will pay for assisted living, but this isn't easy to find and depends on your state's rules. In Massachusetts, this is like finding a needle in a haystack. You will probably need an elder law attorney to assist you. I know a few assisted-living facilities that accept Medicaid benefits to help residents stay, usually after they have already paid a considerable amount of money privately before going on Medicaid.

- **Home Care:** Medicaid will help seniors who meet strict financial requirements pay for home care. Your income and assets must be below a certain limit to qualify. Unfortunately, many seniors who are essentially penniless cannot qualify for these programs because their income is just above the limit. Sometimes, their only option is to go to a nursing home since Medicaid usually does not impose an income limit to pay for nursing home care.

- **Nursing Home Care:** If you have limited resources, Medicaid can cover the cost of nursing home care. To be eligible for benefits, a nursing home resident must have no more than $2,000 in "countable assets." Countable assets can be easily converted to cash, like investments, certain annuities, real estate, retirement accounts, etc. Usually, your primary residence is not considered a countable asset.

Once you start receiving Medicaid benefits, you'll be required to contribute almost all your income towards the cost of the nursing home. In Massachusetts, you can only keep $72.80 monthly for personal needs and enough to cover any supplemental health insurance and sometimes an allowance for your spouse.

Can you protect your assets and receive Medicaid?

The options for protecting assets for single individuals applying for Medicaid benefits to pay for nursing home care are limited. If your assets exceed the $2,000 limit, an elder law attorney can help you determine if you can protect your assets or strategically spend them to benefit you instead of spending all your savings on nursing home care.

If you are married and your spouse needs nursing home care, it is more likely that you will be able to protect assets and qualify for Medicaid benefits. Getting advice from an elder law attorney as early as possible, will give you the best chance of protecting assets.

Here are a few options that may be available to protect your assets if you need to apply for Medicaid benefits:

- **Pooled Disability Trusts:** In some states, there may be an option to establish a "Pooled Disability Trust." This type of Trust is typically managed by a non-profit agency, which acts as the Trustee for an account established for your benefit to help pay for things to improve your quality of life.

For example, the funds may be used for companion services, transportation, haircuts, cable, clothing, personal belongings, shopping services, and other expenditures not covered by Medicaid. This Trust must include a "payback" provision, which directs that Medicaid be reimbursed if any funds remain in the Trust at your death.

- Prepay for your funeral: Prepaying for your funeral is one way to ensure your wishes are carried out and also an excellent way to reduce your assets if you need to apply for Medicaid benefits.

- Pay your debts before spending all of your money on nursing home care and applying for Medicaid benefits.

- Purchase any items you may need, such as furniture, clothing, a television, a new phone, etc.

PACE

No one wants to go to a nursing home. The Program of All-Inclusive Care for the Elderly (PACE) helps seniors receive the support they need to stay out of a nursing home whenever possible. PACE integrates Medicare and Medicaid to provide seniors a wide range of care, allowing them to maintain their independence. It has two main components:

- The first main component involves a day program at a PACE Center with an on-site team of professionals, including doctors, nurses, social workers, and physical therapists. The seniors receive personalized care. PACE provides transportation to the PACE Center, where seniors can participate in activities, eat lunch together, and get the care they need to stay out of a nursing home.

- When a senior also needs help at home, PACE may provide assistance with personal needs, medication management, and chores.

PACE helps seniors stay out of nursing homes and fight loneliness and isolation. In certain instances, PACE helps pay for assisted living facilities. It is currently available in 33 states. It helps seniors receive support, whether they have a strong support network or are aging alone.

How do you get PACE?

The PACE program is free for seniors meeting income and asset requirements. The asset limit is $2,000, and the income limit varies by state. Elder law attorneys are often able to make recommendations to help seniors qualify and protect assets. If you have Medicare Advantage, you won't be able to qualify for PACE, so it is better to switch to regular Medicare.

For those who do not meet the financial requirements, PACE may offer a private pay option.

PACE aims to explore every avenue to enable seniors to remain in their communities and homes. If it becomes necessary for seniors to transition to nursing home care, PACE also provides assistance. I have had many clients who stayed out of a nursing home and received excellent care because of PACE, as was true with Kay.

Kay

I was Kay's guardian. She lived in an assisted-living facility in Boston. Kay was originally from Ireland and had no family in the United States. She had served as a nurse in World War II. She was a sweet woman with a great sense of humor and some very interesting stories.

After paying for the assisted living facility for a few years, Kay was beginning to run out of money, and her only option would be to move to a nursing home. However, I enrolled Kay in the PACE program, which helped her pay for the assisted living facility. In addition, Kay had the option of going to the PACE Center. She loved going there each weekday, where the aides kept her engaged and well cared for. She enjoyed the activities, socialization, special events, entertainment, and support.

Kay was able to stay at the assisted living facility until she died.

Veteran's Programs

Our veterans have made a tremendous sacrifice for our country. While there is no way to compensate them, certain programs assist our aging heroes, such as:

- **Aid and Attendance Benefit (A&A):** Aid and Attendance benefits help certain veterans and their widows/widowers pay for health care needs at home, in an assisted-living facility, or in a nursing home. To qualify, the veteran must have served during wartime. There is an asset limit for this program. To learn more about this program or if you qualify, contact the Veteran's Office in your city or town.

- **"Soldier's Home" Nursing Homes:** Each state has Soldiers' Homes to care for veterans. They offer long term care, physical therapy, hospital care, and social services. The cost of long term care at a Soldier's Home facility is significantly lower than a private long term care facility. This can help preserve assets and allow veterans to get the care they need.

If you are a veteran, I recommend that you reach out to your local Veteran's Affairs Office to determine if there are any services or benefits you may be able to receive.

Using Reverse Mortgages to Pay for Long-Term Care at Home

If you do not have enough money to pay for your care but you own your home, a reverse mortgage can help provide the money you need money to pay for care to help you continue living at home. How does a reverse mortgage work?

A reverse mortgage allows homeowners, ages 62 and older, to receive money in exchange for the equity in their home. This can be a lump sum payment, monthly payments, or a line of credit. Unlike a traditional mortgage, the homeowner only needs to pay something back once they sell the house, move, or die. At that point, the reverse mortgage must be repaid.

If the sale proceeds are higher than the loan balance, the excess funds go to the homeowner or their estate. If the loan balance exceeds the home's value, the homeowner or their estate is generally not responsible for the difference.

If a homeowner uses up all the equity in their home through a reverse mortgage, they will not be forced to sell it if they continue to meet the loan requirements. They can still live in the house without making mortgage payments.

One downside of a reverse mortgage is that the fees and interest rates can be very high. Be sure you understand the financial implications and consult with a reverse mortgage lender and a financial advisor before proceeding with one. You may have other options to help you age in place, such as downsizing or renting out a portion of your home.

• • • •

If you want to prepare yourself for the high cost of long term care, consider your situation and whether you should consult an elder law attorney or financial advisor to give you peace of mind.

PART III: HOUSING, COMMUNITY, AND END-OF-LIFE CARE

11. DECLUTTERING AND DOWNSIZING — DON'T LET YOUR STUFF HOLD YOU BACK

"Letting go of clutter creates room for joy, freedom, and new possibilities."
— *Anonymous*

Decluttering and downsizing may seem like a strange topic to start this part of the book, but one of the greatest lessons I have learned from my clients is how important it is not to let your stuff hold you back.

I have been involved in several cases of extreme hoarding, where my clients' homes were so bad that they could no longer live there. One client spent almost eight months in a homeless shelter after the Board of Health condemned his home, which was full of "collector's items."

Bob

A 96-year-old living alone, Bob would ride his bike daily to the local soup kitchen for lunch. He didn't show up for a few days, and the staff became concerned. They called the police to do a wellness check, and they found him lying on the floor in horrible conditions. He had fallen days earlier.

Bob was a hoarder. His house had only a small path to walk through, covered in garbage, mail, newspapers, bugs, and junk. The Board of Health deemed it unfit for human habitation. Bob stayed at the hospital for a few months while I was appointed Guardian and Conservator.

Bob was happy to go to an assisted-living facility, where he loved the food, especially the ice cream, and being cared for in a safe environment. He seemed perfectly content to be there and never missed his home. Locating his assets and family was one of my most interesting adventures. I had to wear a Hazmat suit to enter Bob's home for my brief visit, accompanied by the Board of Health caseworker. After walking through a tunnel of papers and garbage, I felt like I needed decontamination.

Finding information was impossible in that mess, so I met with the IRS to get some clues about his income, which eventually led to finding Bob's bank and investment accounts, which were surprisingly significant.

A neighbor mentioned that Bob also owned a vacation home. When I asked him about this, he said it sounded familiar but couldn't remember where it was. After conducting a title search, I found the home, which had been abandoned for over 15 years and was so run-down that a raccoon family had moved in.

I also located Bob's son, who hadn't seen his father since he was two years old. He visited Bob frequently until he died and eventually inherited everything.

Although I found this to be one of my most interesting cases, Bob's situation highlights how even a person with significant assets can become a hoarder and run into trouble for failing to plan.

Bob's case may be extreme, but I have met many seniors who wanted to move to a senior living community but could not imagine going to a small one-bedroom apartment. What would they do with all their furniture, clothes, memorabilia, gifts, trinkets, photos, and inherited and treasured possessions they had gathered over the years? As hard as it may be to get rid of these things, if you don't organize and downsize your stuff, someone else eventually will (and without proper legal planning, it will be a stranger).

Even if you plan to stay in your home as you age, someone will deal with your stuff after you pass away. This person will probably sell items worth more than $1,000, but most of your possessions will likely be disposed of or donated. Your photos may be thrown away if you don't have family to take them.

Isn't it better to organize your belongings, keep what you need and care about, and get rid of the rest? You may want to give some things to friends or neighbors now or donate them to charity. Giving away items while you are alive can be very rewarding. Perhaps you have something that your friend would love. By giving it to them now, you can see how much it is appreciated and feel the joy of giving.

The Importance of Decluttering

While not everyone is a hoarder, it's incredible how much stuff most of us accumulate without even realizing it. We all have that moment when we open a closet or a drawer, and suddenly, it hits us—there's just so much! It can feel overwhelming. The average American home contains 300,000 items. A recent survey found that one in four Americans has a clutter problem.

Our possessions are more than just "things." They hold memories, hopes, or even regrets. While keeping items that remind us of the past is comforting, they can also weigh us down emotionally. Research shows that clutter can contribute to stress and anxiety. But here's the good news: decluttering can bring a sense of relief and control. It clears not just your physical space but your mental space, too.

Tips for Decluttering

So, how do you start? There's no shortage of books, YouTube videos, and expert advice from professional organizers. You can even ask a friend for support or hire a professional if you feel stuck. But here are a few simple tips:

- **Start Small:** Focus on one small area for 15-30 minutes to avoid feeling overwhelmed. Tackle a different section each week.

- **Sort and Label:** Use boxes labeled "Keep," "Donate," and "Trash." Group items by category, like clothes or kitchenware, for easier organization.

- **Follow the One-Year Rule:** If you haven't used it in the past year, consider letting it go. Be selective with sentimental items.

- **Take a Picture:** Struggling to part with something? Take a photo to preserve the memory.

- **Tackle Paperwork:** Recycle old papers, magazines, and junk mail. Scan important documents for digital storage.

- **Plan for Estate Distribution:** Create a list of cherished items to pass on to loved ones or charities. Keep it with your estate planning documents, or even better, give it to them now unless you need it.

- **Consider Storage:** If you're not ready to let go but don't have space for it, rent storage space for peace of mind—but storage costs add up. Is it worth it?

Imagine living in a home that feels open, light, and filled with only the things that truly matter to you. What a reward for the hard task of decluttering.

The Advantages of Downsizing

Once you declutter, you might prefer living in a smaller home or a senior living community with amenities. Downsizing offers several advantages, such as reduced maintenance costs, less cleaning, and improved accessibility if your health needs change. Moving to a new home can provide a fresh start in an environment that better aligns with your current needs and preferences.

While you can stay in your home as long as your health and finances allow, it is wise to be prepared to move if needed. This means getting rid of a great deal of stuff now, a process that is easier when done little by little.

• • • •

It can be overwhelming to make so many changes at once, so do what you must to keep your sanity. As hard as leaving your home and getting rid of your stuff may be, it can also be freeing. It will allow you to move into the next chapter of your life or choose a housing option that makes sense for you.

12. HOUSING: EXPLORE SUITABLE LIVING ARRANGEMENTS

*"You may feel like home is the anchor in your storm,
but leaving may well save you from drowning."*
— *Unknown*

Many people prefer the peace and quiet of being alone. However, loneliness can be difficult. It's not just the lack of companionship that can be challenging, but also the feeling of insecurity. Questions like, "What if I fall or get sick and no one knows about it?" can keep you up at night.

As we age, it becomes crucial to consider the practical aspects of where we live to ensure that our needs will be met if our circumstances or physical or mental health change. Fortunately, there are options to provide solo seniors with social connections, safety, and support. Choosing the one that works best for you is key to preserving your autonomy and independence. This chapter will provide an overview of housing options recommended for solo seniors.

Evaluate Your Current Living Situation

Choosing where you will live is one of the most important decisions. This one decision can impact your quality of life, independence, and overall well-being in the future and make it possible for you to thrive. Start by evaluating your current living situation. Here are some things to consider:

• Are you happy with your current living situation?

• Will your current house still work if you need more support?

- Is it too big, hard to maintain, or missing key accessibility features like a first-floor bathroom?

- A home that requires major changes may not be ideal if you want to continue living there.

- If you plan to stay in your current home, should you start renovating now? How much time and cost would be involved? Can you afford this?

- Even if you modified your house, do you have enough money to pay for the help you need to stay there safely as your needs change?

- It is also important to consider the emotional aspects, such as feelings of isolation or safety concerns, when deciding whether you should stay in your home.

It will be too late if you wait for a crisis to think about this. It will likely take time to set up a situation where you can safely stay in your own home, like in Mike's case:

Mike

Mike had Parkinson's disease, and it was getting harder for him to take care of himself at home as he was having difficulty walking. He was in a terrible pattern, where he would fall, go to a hospital, spend a few weeks in short-term rehabilitation, and then return to his apartment. His adult son lived far away and could not help. During one hospitalization, he called me asking for help.

Mike did not have enough money to pay for home care for the long term. I helped him protect his limited assets, $50,000, by establishing a Pooled Disability Trust and applying for Medicaid benefits to pay for nursing home care.

Mike was not ready to give up on returning to his apartment. Even though he was in a nursing home, he kept paying the rent at his apartment. I hired a geriatric care manager to determine if there was any way to help him move back home. His apart-

ment was not handicapped-accessible, and he needed to use a wheelchair. The geriatric care manager helped Mike get on a waiting list for a handicapped-accessible apartment. After over one year in the nursing home, an apartment became available. Mike moved into the apartment with private home care for a very short time until we got him approved for PACE, a Medic-aid-funded program.

The PACE transportation picked him up each weekday. It brought him to the center, where he enjoyed activities, entertainment, and lunch. In addition, they provided a home health aide to help with personal care needs for a few hours each day at home. It took a long time, but Mike was happy that he could live in his apartment again.

In the end, everything worked out for Mike, but if he had been more proactive, he could have avoided going to the nursing home for over a year, which was very hard for him.

Aging in Place

In the past, seniors often lived at home until they could not; and then the only choice was a nursing home. Today, many alternatives give seniors more flexibility to meet their needs. Here, we explore the options for aging in place, which means living in your own home:

Staying in your Home

Planning will give you the best odds of success if you want to stay in your own home. As your needs change, you may need to modify your bathroom by installing grab bars or a bench to sit on in the shower and removing a bathtub that could be difficult to climb. If your stairs become challenging, you can install a stair lift or ramps. You should be prepared to hire caregivers, housekeepers, landscapers, repairmen, and others to assist in maintaining your safety and your home.

Aging in place can be very expensive. You can make this work with enough money to pay for whatever you need. However, if you cannot afford the renovations or care, a reverse mortgage (discussed in Chapter 9: Planning for Health Care and Long term Care Costs) could help. Alternatively, you can find other creative ways to stay, such as sharing your home to reduce expenses.

Sharing Housing Options

Sharing housing and expenses is a wonderful way for solo seniors, to have companionship. Here are a few home-sharing ideas to consider:

- **Sharing with another senior:** Several websites, such as SeniorHomeShares.com and Silvernest.com, help seniors find others interested in sharing housing. This is a creative and affordable idea. If you are considering this option, please carefully screen potential roommates. I recommend a background check on potential roommates and getting to know them before moving in together.

- **Sharing with a younger person:** Another option may be to have a younger person live with you and help you in exchange for reduced rent. Nesterly.com is one way of finding a tenant. This website helps to connect you with a younger person who can help with household chores, companionship, and errands. Although, they won't help with personal care needs. Nesterly conducts background checks and requires references for all tenants. They also take care of the rental agreements and collect the rent.

- **Sharing with a friend:** Moving in with a friend or group of friends can be a great way to stay connected and save money. It worked for the Golden Girls and could work for you, too. As you need more help, you can share the costs of caregiving. It is important to consider the financial implications and create a written agreement outlining the expectations and financial arrangements for your living expenses. You should contact an Elder Law or Real Estate attorney to draft this agreement and help you consider its potential consequences.

- **Buying a home together:** If you are considering buying a house with a friend or family member instead of renting, it may be best to create a Trust to hold the title. You will need to hire an Elder Law or Real Estate attorney to help you think about what will happen if one of you dies or moves out and to protect any equity you may have against Medicaid liens.

Community Living

If keeping up with a house feels like too much work, or if you're ready to start a new and exciting chapter, community living could be a great option. There are different types that offer a range of lifestyle options, amenities, and levels of support.

Independent Living Communities

These communities are designed for seniors who are healthy, active, and able to care for themselves but want the benefits of living in a vibrant community. You have your own space, like an apartment, condo, or townhouse, while enjoying extras like housekeeping, social events, transportation, maintenance, and meals.

Many seniors love the sense of community these places offer. Options range from small, cozy settings to large, lively campuses with plenty of activities and amenities—almost like a college campus for older adults.

The cost depends on where the community is, their services, and your living space size. Prices usually start around $3,000 per month) for the basics, and luxury living can cost $10,000 monthly or more in expensive areas. Some places also have a one-time entrance fee, ranging from $50,000 to $500,000 or more.

Independent living is a fantastic option if you don't want the responsibility of maintaining a house and are ready to start a new chapter in your life.

Affordable Senior Housing

If price is a concern, affordable senior housing is a great option. These are age-restricted apartments, typically for people 60 and older, subsidized through federal, state, and local government programs and non-profit organizations.

Almost all towns have affordable apartments for seniors who meet specific financial requirements. Usually, the rent will be one-third of your income. Most Senior Housing apartments provide social support and activities to the residents. If you need care for personal needs, you may qualify for home care paid by Medicaid.

Affordable Senior Housing is a low-cost way to live in a safe community that may provide some support as your circumstances change. There are often waitlists that may be over one year long. If you are interested in this option, put your name on the list now as soon as possible. You can always change your mind when your name comes up.

Assisted Living Facilities

Assisted Living Facilities are similar to Independent Living Communities, with private apartments and access to amenities. However, they also provide extra support for seniors who need help with personal care, medication management, meals, and housekeeping. These communities are ideal for those who need assistance while still having their own space.

The cost of assisted living varies based on the care and services you need. The national average starts at about $5,000 monthly, though prices can be much higher in certain areas.

Many facilities also charge a one-time entrance fee, which can significantly increase the cost.

When exploring your options, it's essential to understand the services offered and ensure they meet your needs. Most facilities will have you meet with a nurse to assess your care requirements and create a service plan. Being realistic about the care you need and whether the facility can provide it is important. The amount of care assisted living facilities offer ranges depending on the facility.

One of my clients learned this the hard way. She moved into an Assisted Living Facility, but after just two nights, it became clear that the facility couldn't meet her needs. Unfortunately, the facility had a non-refundable $5,000 community fee. It required sixty days' notice to terminate the contract, which meant they charged her $15,000 for just two nights. It wasn't until I intervened as her attorney and threatened legal action that they refunded most of her money. Without an advocate, she might not have recovered these costs.

This experience highlights the importance of carefully evaluating Assisted Living Facilities before committing. Ask plenty of questions, review the contract closely, and make sure you fully understand the terms, including fees and cancellation policies. Planning ahead can save you stress and unexpected expenses later.

Continuing Care Retirement Communities (CCRCs)

Continuing Care Retirement Communities typically offer Independent Living, Assisted Living, Memory Care, and Skilled Nursing Home services on the same campus. This is a wonderful option for seniors interested in a community where they can age in place. Many seniors in their 70s think they are too young for this. However, moving into an Independent Living apartment while you are still active gives you a chance to make friends, enjoy an easier lifestyle with at least one meal per day, and not worry about maintenance.

If you need more care as you age, these communities are ready to provide for your needs. It is helpful to stay on the same campus, as you will likely make friends, and you can continue to see them as your needs or theirs change.

It is best to visit several communities before deciding. There are many interesting and vibrant options. You may be surprised at how nice they are. You will have your own apartment, kitchen, and privacy, but you will be in a supportive setting that will adjust to your needs if they change. Moving to a Continuing Care Retirement Community is a fantastic option for seniors planning on aging alone.

The only downside is that it can be expensive. Some communities require a hefty upfront fee, plus monthly rent, before moving in ($300,000 or more). The fee is usually mostly refundable when you move out or die. Others only require monthly rent, usually at $4,000 and often much higher.

Some communities are willing to negotiate on the price. If there is a community that you are interested in, but it is slightly too expensive for you, let them know that you cannot quite afford it. Name your price, and see if they are willing to accept it. If you feel uncomfortable negotiating the price, you could hire an elder law attorney or work with a Senior Living Advisor to help you. Before you sign an agreement, it is helpful for an attorney to review the paperwork for any potential red flags.

Ideally, you want to move into a community where you can stay for many years. If you are unsure if you will have enough money to stay there until the end of your life, be sure to ask the facility what will happen if your money runs out. Some facilities have financial programs to help you stay. This should be a top factor for seniors with limited funds when choosing a community.

Even though you think you may not be ready or too young, it is best to move into a community while you are still vibrant and able to participate and engage with others. If you wait for a crisis or a decline, it will be much harder.

Nursing Homes

The nursing home is the last resort. No one wants to go to a nursing home unless their needs cannot be met in a different setting. Unfortunately, there are circumstances when it is the only option. As difficult as this may be to accept, ensuring that you are safe and that your needs are met is the top priority

In a nursing home, you will have a private or shared room. There will be around-the-clock nursing care, assistance with eating, bathing, dressing, and mobility, rehabilitation services, social activities, specialized care for conditions like Alzheimer's or dementia, meals, laundry, and more.

Tips on How to Be Proactive If a Nursing Home Becomes Necessary

- **Learn about the nursing homes in your area:** Even though you may never need one, I recommend you learn about the nursing homes in your area now. Talk to friends, social workers, elder law attorneys, or anyone with experience with nursing homes. You can also look at online reviews. Visit Medicare's website to compare different nursing homes: www.medicare.gov/care-compare.

- **Visit:** You can visit a nursing home well before needing one. Just call the Admissions Director and request a tour.

- **Make a list:** If you ever have a medical event and go to the hospital, there will be little time to decide which nursing home you will go to when you are discharged. As soon

---

as you are medically stable, the hospital will want you to leave and will only give you a day or so to figure out where you will go. Knowing a few nursing homes in your area will help ensure you go to a higher-quality place. If you have a professional acting as your Health Care Proxy or Power of Attorney, they should be able to help you figure this out, or you can hire a Geriatric Care Manager to help you. Once you leave the hospital, you will likely stay in the facility where you are placed for the long term.

- **Hire a Private Companion:** Even the best nursing homes are short-staffed. Hiring a private companion to visit you as often as possible will ensure you receive the highest quality of care.

  They may sit with you, take you out for a walk, or out to lunch. Having this help can make a huge difference in your life. Also, if the nurses know you have someone checking in on you regularly, they are more likely to give you excellent care. If no one is checking, they may put your needs last.

- **Create a Pooled Disability Trust:** If you have limited resources, please refer to the section in this book discussing Pooled Disability Trusts (Chapter 9: Planning for Health Care and Long term Care Costs). This type of Trust is managed by an agency, which acts as the Trustee for an account established for your benefit to help pay for things to improve your quality of life. The funds in the Trust are used for things like private companions, additional therapy, a new wheelchair, etc.

Creative Ideas for the Future

We need new and creative approaches to support solo seniors. Approximately 27% of Americans over 65 live alone. Living alone increases the risk of poverty, health issues, and isolation. The good news is that new and creative senior living options are emerging. While they may not be as common as the ones discussed earlier in this chapter, you may find one or two worth exploring further:

- **Co-Housing Communities**: In these resident-driven neighborhoods, people own their homes while sharing common spaces like kitchens and gardens, focusing on collaboration and independence. Co-housing is available in various states, such as California, Colorado, and Massachusetts.

- **Village Movement:** The Village Movement enables seniors to stay in their homes while paying an annual membership fee ($300-$1,500) for services like transportation, home repairs, and social activities. The model is community-based, with villages run by seniors, volunteers, or staff. Some villages offer sliding scale fees, financial assistance for low-income seniors, and home care at additional costs. Inspired by Beacon Hill Village in Boston, villages are expanding. There are hundreds across America. To find one near you, visit https://www.vtvnetwork.org.

- **Agrihoods:** These neighborhoods are built around shared farms or gardens. The focus on nature and community supports physical and mental well-being. Agrihoods are typically found in California, Georgia, and Colorado. The cost of living in agrihoods varies widely, ranging from $300,000 to over $1 million for homes.

- **Tiny Home Communities:** Specifically designed for seniors, these communities provide low-maintenance living with shared amenities like communal gardens, activity centers, and support services. They are becoming popular, particularly in Texas, Florida, Oregon, California, and Colorado. A tiny home costs $30,000 to $150,000, with monthly lot fees ranging from $300 to $700.

- **Intergenerational Care Communities:** In these communities, seniors live near childcare centers or schools in these communities, encouraging meaningful interactions between seniors and younger generations. Some models pair senior housing with daycare centers so older adults can engage with children through storytelling, mentoring, or shared activities. Newbridge on the Charles, in Massachusetts, is a Continuing Care Retirement Community on the same campus as a school, providing opportunities for the two communities to interact.

• • • •

Until more creative senior living options become widely available, my best advice is to take the time now to understand your options and choose one that works best for you. Whether you are thinking about staying in your home or in an independent living community, or you are interested in one of the newer models, planning ahead is key to preserving your independence and thriving.

13. STAYING ENGAGED AND FINDING COMMUNITY

"Alone, we can do so little;
together, we can do so much."
— Helen Keller

Social isolation can have a serious effect on both mental and physical health. Not only is loneliness a major risk factor for depression and anxiety in older adults, but it can also accelerate cognitive impairment. A study by the Alzheimer's Association found that seniors who engage in regular social activities have a 70% lower rate of cognitive decline compared to those who are socially isolated.

Before she passed away at age 96, the Governor of New York appointed Dr. Ruth Westheimer as the State's Loneliness Ambassador. The well-known sex therapist, media personality, author, and Holocaust survivor advocated for combating loneliness, emphasizing that social connections and a support system are essential at any age.

Dr. Ruth encouraged people to reach out to others and build friendships rather than waiting for others to do so. "Loneliness is not a reality; it's a feeling. Feelings can be changed by other feelings," Dr. Ruth explained. These "other feelings"—motivation, fulfillment, optimism, self-worth, confidence, belonging, and happiness—arise from having a sense of purpose.

Rekindling a Sense of Purpose

As we age, all the activities that come with jobs, families, and other obligations dwindle, and they can feel either liberating or empty. I believe that having "things to do, places to go, and people to see" is one of the keys to thriving. While friendships and social connections play a critical role, equally important—if not more—is what people describe as the feeling of "being useful," achieved by working and helping others.

Keep working

Work gives you a sense of purpose and something to do every day. Feeling useful and needed keeps us going. Many seniors continue to work well past the traditional retirement age. Famous examples include Donald Trump, Joe Biden, Warren Buffet, Clint Eastwood, Betty White, and Dolly Parton.

Dolly Parton

At the age of 78, after a career spanning more than 50 years, the country music legend says that she hopes to drop dead on stage. "I will never retire unless I have to. As long as I'm able to get up in the morning, get that makeup on and my high heels on, and even if I can't wear high heels, I'm going to do like Mae West, I'm going to sit in a wheelchair with my high heels on,".

If you are working and enjoying it, keep going for as long as possible. If you put in too many hours or you don't like your job, consider looking for part-time, seasonal, or more flexible work. A wonderful organization called Seniors Helping Seniors provides companionship and home care to people who need help. A job like this offers a source of income, social interaction, and the opportunity to help others. For more information, visit: https://seniorshelpingseniors.com.

Help others

Making a difference is a great way to have a meaningful life and fight loneliness. Many inspiring seniors contribute their time, energy, and love to the world, but one of my favorites is the man who came to be known as the "ICU Grandpa."

David Deutchman

David Deutchman had a successful career, but his work post-retirement defined his legacy. Before he died in 2020, he spent 14 years as a "baby buddy," volunteering to hold sick and premature babies in the hospital. This is how he describes the experience and the benefits, both for the babies and himself:

"Some of my guy friends don't understand it. I get peed on. I get puked on. I mean, why wouldn't I love it?" "It is very gratifying, not just because the babies are crying and you help them to stop crying. There are many benefits to that warm connection of being held—when a baby puts their face against your heartbeat, there's a benefit there. I came to love it, not just because of the connection with the babies, but the whole atmosphere of the hospital."

David's presence provided comfort and support for the babies, their families, and hospital staff. David is a legend who touched many lives. His story is a powerful reminder of the impact one person can have through simple acts of kindness and compassion.

Ideas for Helping Others

Making a positive impact can be deeply fulfilling. Here are some ways to get involved:

- **Support your neighbors:** Offer childcare assistance or be a reliable and friendly neighbor.

- **Volunteer locally**: Help at hospitals, nursing homes, food pantries, or schools. Many libraries also match volunteers with individuals learning English.

- **Support causes you care about:** Get involved in environmental, educational, or community initiatives.

- **Help seniors:** Volunteer through programs to assist older adults with daily tasks or social connections.

- **Engage with organizations:** Contribute to charities like Cradles to Crayons or Horizons for Homeless in Boston, which provide essential services for children and families.

Sharing your time and talents enriches the lives of others and brings a sense of purpose and joy to your own.

Building Local Networks for Solo Seniors

I am exploring ways to help solo seniors connect with one another and form small, local networks of support. These groups can provide a trusted circle of peers in your area—people to offer both social and practical support.

If you're interested in joining, leading, or helping to organize a local solo aging group, I invite you to visit www.soloallies.com and complete a short form. If enough people express interest in your region, I will do my best to connect you with others who share the same goal.

Many of you have unique talents, energy, and enthusiasm that can help bring this idea to life. How wonderful would it be if we could build a network of solo seniors supporting one another? If this idea resonates with you, take the first step—visit the website and let's see what we can create together!

Staying Engaged

Remaining active and connected is vital for well-being. Here are some ideas:

- **Join a community group:** Explore options like the Village to Village Network, which offers seniors social events and practical support to help seniors live at home for an affordable fee.

- **Stay physically active:** Participate in group exercises, pickleball, or gardening to promote health and connection.

- **Pursue hobbies:** Join crafting, book clubs, or art classes to keep your mind stimulated and meet like-minded people.

- **Volunteer remotely:** Use your skills to mentor, tutor, or support causes virtually from home.

- **Explore new interests:** Try blogging, podcasting, or creating content to share your insights and engage with others.

- **Keep learning:** Take classes at a local community center or online. Many programs cater specifically to older adults.

- **Travel if you can:** Join solo travel groups or participate in international volunteer trips, such as those offered by the Peace Corps for older adults.

Connecting as an Introvert

Even introverts can feel the sting of loneliness sometimes. Building meaningful relationships and maintaining social connections doesn't have to feel overwhelming. The key is to show up. Participating in organized activities can make socializing easier—such as joining a book club, where discussions revolve around shared interests, or a crafting group, where the focus is on the activity. As mentioned earlier if you are interested in joining forming a local group of solo seniors, please visit www.soloallies.com to complete a short form to gauge interest and help connect you to others. A few close, meaningful friendships can provide the support and companionship needed to combat feelings of isolation. If reaching out feels daunting, start by connecting with one person who shares your interests or values.

• • • •

Building relationships, staying active, and pursuing lifelong learning can significantly enhance your quality of life as you age. Whether joining a community, picking up new hobbies, or traveling, there are many ways to remain connected. These activities promote a sense of contentment, purpose, and curiosity, all of which help cultivate a positive mindset—a factor so important that I've dedicated the entire next chapter to it.

14. ATTITUDE IS EVERYTHING

"Life is an echo. What you send out, comes back.
What you sow, you reap. What you give, you get.
What you see in others, exists in you."
— Zig Ziglar

Over the years, I have had the privilege of meeting many solo seniors. While their circumstances vary widely, one factor makes all the difference: attitude. Those who are kind and friendly are like magnets—the love and positive energy they radiate are appreciated and returned. Unfortunately, those with poor attitudes often experience greater isolation, unhappiness, and struggle more than necessary.

The Consequences of a Poor Attitude

Aging can be tough, especially if you begin to lose your independence and need to rely on more support from caregivers and professionals. While it's normal to experience emotional ups and downs, good and bad days, allowing these feelings to dominate and lashing out at others can have serious consequences.

I have been involved in cases where caregivers and professionals, eager to help at first, eventually withdraw due to mistreatment. This can make aging in place nearly impossible, as private caregivers may quit and refuse to return. In some cases, nursing home care becomes the only option because finding caregivers willing to work with difficult individuals is so challenging. Even in nursing homes, staff are there to help, not to endure mistreatment, and those with a negative demeanor often find themselves more isolated and unhappy. Sadly, a poor attitude can also limit access to higher-quality facilities, leaving people in less desirable ones. Ultimately, a negative attitude creates a self-fulfilling cycle of loneliness and decline, making everything harder than it needs to be.

Identifying and Addressing a Poor Attitude

Our mindset has a powerful effect on how we experience life and relate to others. While everyone has bad days, allowing negativity to dominate does not help. Recognizing and shifting unhelpful patterns is key to improving well-being.

Ask yourself:

- Do I focus more on problems than solutions?
- Am I open to change and help from others, or do I resist it?
- Do I express gratitude and kindness to those around me?
- Am I quick to criticize, complain, or blame others?

If you see room for improvement, try to change. Start by looking for the good in your day, practice gratitude, and be kind to yourself and others. A positive attitude makes life better. As Walt Whitman wisely said, "Keep your face always toward the sunshine, and shadows will fall behind you."

Stories of Inspiring Solo Seniors

Aging is not just about the challenges we face but also the strength, wisdom, and joy we gather along the way. This section highlights those who embraced challenges with resilience and positivity, demonstrating that thriving is not about avoiding obstacles but navigating them gracefully.

Over the past 25 years of being an elder law attorney, I have met many solo seniors who have inspired me with their positivity, resilience, hope, and faith. I want to share the stories of a few who come to mind as examples of what it means to thrive, even when facing challenges.

Eleanor

Eleanor left a lasting impression on me. She was kind and caring, always with a smile on her face. She was the last one living in her large family, but she embraced everyone she met with a positive attitude. She was full of love, peace, and goodness. Her faith in God and ability to adapt to changes in her life made her a joy to be around. She may not have been famous or made history, but she made an impact on those around her. She taught me that a life filled with love and a positive attitude is well-lived.

Joan

Joan was married and had grown adult children who no longer lived close by. After her husband passed away, Joan made a bold decision to move to Central America during the height of the COVID-19 pandemic to run a school for underprivileged children. Joan didn't let the loss of her spouse or the challenges of living in a foreign country deter her from pursuing her passions. She embraced life with open arms and made a significant difference in the lives of the children she helped. Joan's story is a testament to the power of resilience and the impact one can make when approaching life with courage and determination. Her bravery and sense of adventure is inspiring.

Debbie

I met Debbie while learning to play pickleball. She was much better than I was, but she took the time to practice with me to help me improve. Debbie had a positive and fun attitude. She told me that after her husband died, she decided to move to Florida. She didn't let grief hold her back; instead, she wrote a book, made new friends, volunteered, and kept a positive outlook. Debbie's children were not actively involved in her life, but she didn't let that stop her from creating a fulfilling life. She approached life with a positive attitude.

Tricia

One of my clients, Tricia, was another senior who exemplified the power of a positive attitude. In her 70s, she learned how to sail and got involved with Ballroom dancing, which brought her great joy. Tricia's enthusiasm for life was infectious, and she showed me that it's never too late to pursue new interests and live life to the fullest. She had a joyful way about her that others appreciated.

Leo

Leo was a retired engineer in his early 70s who had spent most of his life planning and preparing for every possible outcome. Understandably, he was grieving the loss of his wife, who had been by his side for over 50 years. He never expected to be alone at a relatively young age.

Recently, Leo came to see me about updating his estate planning documents. I hadn't seen him in a few years. He wanted to update his documents because he was about to get married. He had met a wonderful woman while walking his beloved dogs. Leo decided to embrace change with an open heart, and I could see how happy he was.

His approach to life after his wife's passing was rooted in believing that every ending is a new beginning. He focused on what he could do rather than what he had lost. His story is a powerful reminder that life's challenges can be met with grace and that it's never too late to bring new people into our lives.

George and Lucy

Of course, not everyone is physically able to participate in activities like pickleball, sailing, or ballroom dancing. I have met many clients who face serious physical challenges and rely on others for their most basic needs. Two of the most memorable clients I had were George and Lucy. They both had debilitating multiple sclerosis (MS), which they were diagnosed with when they were in their forties. By the time I met them, they were both quadriplegics. I would meet with them at their small apartment, where they needed the assistance of caregivers 24 hours a day.

They met at the MS support group, fell in love, and married. They supported each other through a devastating diagnosis, and over several years, they lost their physical ability to care for themselves. However, it was evident to anyone who met them that they never lost their passion for life, joy, love, and caring for each other.

I looked forward to meeting with them and helping them ensure their estate planning documents were prepared. I also helped them navigate applying for public benefit programs to pay for their costly care and allow them to live in their own homes rather than being forced to move to a nursing home.

George and Lucy told me about their lives before MS and showed me pictures. They had successful careers, enjoyed sports, and were both beautiful. MS may have taken away their physical abilities, but they found new things to appreciate. They were together until the end, surrounded by love, and died within weeks of each other. They taught me there is always something to smile about, even when challenges are great.

These inspiring individuals remind us that it's never too late to learn, grow, or reinvent ourselves. Their journeys illustrate that aging well isn't about perfection but embracing life's changes and making the most of every moment. I am sure you have met inspiring people in your life. What can you learn from them and try to model as you embrace your future?

• • • •

I am grateful to my clients, who taught me many life lessons. Sometimes, it can be challenging to keep a positive attitude and be grateful. I know that all I can do is ask God for strength to remember the many blessings in life and be thankful for them.

15. END-OF-LIFE CARE

"Oh Wow, oh Wow, oh Wow!"
— *Steve Jobs's last words*

The only certainty in life is that it ends. What is most important is how we live it. We can't always control our circumstances, but we can control our choices and actions. As we have seen in the previous chapter, a poor attitude makes things worse, while positivity helps us move forward with grace until the end.

We all know that death is certain. Sometimes, the way we die is completely out of our control, and in other cases, we can decide the care and comfort we want to receive at the end of our lives. End-of-life care provides comfort, dignity, and support to those in the final stages of life. In this chapter, we will discuss the available resources that help make the end of our lives as peaceful as possible.

Celebrating Life and Finding Closure

Some people are not afraid of dying, especially if they have faith in God or other religious beliefs. If you need support in this area, psychologists, psychiatrists, grief counselors, death doulas, and social workers can offer professional insights and therapeutic approaches. Support groups can also provide solace and perspectives from others facing similar challenges. Religious leaders can offer comfort by helping you find meaning and peace through faith.

Gaining a sense of control over the inevitable can foster acceptance and peace. If planning brings you comfort and a sense of empowerment, consider these thoughtful steps to bring closure and honor, and celebrate your life.

- **Choose a Burial Type:** Whether you prefer a traditional burial, cremation, green burial, water cremation, or body donation, selecting an option that aligns with your values allows you to express your beliefs. For example, a green burial or memorial tree planting symbolizes a return to nature, while a body donation reflects a commitment to science and learning.

- **Pre-Arrange Your Funeral:** Also known as a "Pre-Need Contract" or "Prepaid Funeral Plan," this option allows you to plan and pay for services in advance, easing the financial and emotional burden at the end of your life for those you care about.

- **Plan a Symbolic Act:** Symbolic gestures, such as scattering ashes in a location that holds meaning for you, can help foster acceptance and mark the final chapter of your journey. Other meaningful acts include creating a memory garden, commissioning a memorial bench or plaque, releasing lanterns or butterflies, or crafting keepsakes from remains.

- **Write a Legacy Letter:** Also known as an "Ethical Will" or "Letter of Life Lessons," this personal statement allows you to share your values and life lessons. Writing a Legacy Letter can provide emotional closure and offer peace of mind by ensuring that what was most meaningful to you is preserved.

- **Write Your Life Story:** Many resources—writing software, voice-to-text apps, digital storytelling tools, and self-publishing platforms—make this accessible. For personalized support, ghostwriters, editors, oral historians, and memory coaches can help you structure and capture your memories.

- **Create a Memory Book:** A memory book, like a scrapbook, collects written narratives, photos, drawings, letters, and other mementos. For those who enjoy cooking, a recipe book with family favorites and traditional dishes can be a beautiful legacy.

- **Record Personal Messages for Loved Ones:** Video or audio messages allow you to share memories, gratitude, and encouragement for loved ones.

- **Create a Legacy Project:** Some may wish to leave a legacy through charitable work or a community project, like setting up a small scholarship fund, planting a tree in a local park, or donating a favorite book collection to a community library.

These end-of-life plans and legacy projects foster a sense of control and create a lasting celebration of your life. They offer peace as you consider another essential question: How much do you wish to prolong life?

Prolonging Life or Choosing to Go

Medicine has advanced to the point that machines can keep people alive artificially, even though they cannot engage in life, speak, or respond in any meaningful way. They prolong death. Some people want to have every medical intervention possible. I believe that the quality of your life is more important than the quantity. In his final days, my father taught me his last lesson: "Live your life to the fullest, but when you are at the end, do not fight death. Trust in your faith in God."

My Father

My dad died at 77 years old. One year earlier, he had been sick with pneumonia, which took a toll on him. Before this, he had always been very healthy. He ran a few miles each day until he was in his late 60s. After his annual physical, he would proudly tell me how low his cholesterol levels were or how great his blood pressure was.

After the pneumonia, his health declined significantly. When his kidneys began to fail, he decided to forgo dialysis or any aggres-

sive measures to help him stay alive. He chose to go into hospice care. My father was a Christian with a deep faith in God. He was not afraid of dying. He was grateful for his life, proud that he had reached his life expectancy of 77 years old, and instead of struggling to stay alive, he chose to die peacefully.

I sat by his bedside during his final days. Hospice did an excellent job of keeping him comfortable and supporting our family. My father was not the type to say long goodbyes. If he were at a party, he would quickly say goodbye to the host and leave quietly. That is how he chose to die, and he did it on his terms.

In my role as Guardian, I have had to make decisions about end-of-life care, often without knowing what the person would have wanted. In Massachusetts and many other states, when a person has a court-appointed Guardian, life-sustaining treatment must be provided unless the Guardian obtains a court order providing for comfort measures only, a "Do Not Resuscitate" or "Do Not Intubate" order from the court. This is why planning is critical, especially if you do not want to prolong your life artificially.

In Chapter 3, Health Care Directives, I discussed documents you can create to guide your Health Care Proxy and health care providers about the life-prolonging treatments you do or do not wish to receive.

Your Health Care Proxy and Advanced Directives will be critical at the end of life. Although these were discussed in greater detail in Chapter 2 and Chapter 3, here is a quick recap of these vital documents.

Advanced Directives and End-of-Life Planning

An Advanced Directive is a legal document expressing your wishes for medical care if you cannot communicate them yourself. It may cover treatments like life support and resuscitation and can guide your Health Care Proxy. While not always legally binding, it helps ensure decisions align with your values.

Other helpful documents include:

- **DNR (Do Not Resuscitate) Order:** A directive instructing medical staff not to perform CPR if your heart stops, usually only for the frail or sick.

- **POLST (Physician Orders for Life-Sustaining Treatment):** A medical order specifying the level of care you desire in a medical emergency, signed with a health care provider.

Please review and update these documents any time your health or wishes change.

Professional End-of-Life Care

When no more medical interventions can be offered, or you do not wish to have them, the goal is to be as comfortable as possible in those last months or weeks of life. During this time, palliative care, hospice care, and end of life doulas can provide compassionate and professional support.

Palliative Care

Palliative care is designed to relieve symptoms, pain, and stress. The goal is to improve the patient's quality of life by addressing physical, emotional, social, and spiritual needs. Unlike hospice care, it can be provided alongside treatment. Available in settings like hospitals, outpatient clinics, nursing homes, and sometimes n the patient's home, palliative care is integrated into the patient's overall treatment plan.

Hospice Care

Hospice care provides assistance, support, and comfort in the final stages of a terminal illness when a patient has decided to end treatment. The primary goal is to enhance the patient's quality of life rather than artificially prolong it. Hospice focuses on pain management through palliative care, a tailored care plan from an interdisciplinary team of doctors, nurses, social workers, counselors, and chaplains, and support with practical needs.

Hospice care is available in various settings like the patient's home, hospice centers, hospitals, or nursing homes. To qualify a patient typically requires a terminal diagnosis with a life expectancy of six months or less. Regulations for Hospice care vary by state, affecting eligibility and available services. To understand the options in your area, you can consult a hospice provider or state health department. Hospice care is usually covered by Medicare, Medicaid, private insurance, and veterans' benefits, with some support also offered by some charitable organizations.

Hospice is an incredible resource that offers a holistic approach to care, focused on relieving pain and addressing emotional and spiritual needs. One of its greatest benefits is its focus on dignity and quality of life. It helps people exit with dignity. I have always been impressed by the tremendous care my clients and my father received from hospice.

End-of-Life Doulas

End-of-life or death doulas provide compassionate, non-medical support to individuals and their families during the final stages of life. These trained professionals focus on emotional, spiritual, and practical care. They provide providing comfort and companionship to ensure no one feels alone.

While doulas do not provide medical care, their presence brings reassurance during a deeply personal time. Some hospice programs may include similar services through staff or volunteers, though insurance typically does not cover these.

• • • •

None of us know what the end of our lives will be like. By understanding the decisions that may need to be made and communicating your wishes through a Health Care Directive—if you wish to do so—you will be prepared for whatever lies ahead. I hope you will live a long, healthy life to the fullest and find peace at the end.

16. THRIVING SOLO: PUTTING IT ALL TOGETHER

As we reach the final chapter of *The Solo Senior's Guide to Thrive*, I want to emphasize the core message of this book:

> *Planning + People = Peace of Mind* ™

This simple formula holds the key to a fulfilling, secure, and resilient future for solo seniors.

The word thrive is powerful—it means to grow, flourish, and succeed despite challenges. It represents a journey, not just a destination. Thriving as a solo senior means embracing proactive planning and fostering meaningful connections, ensuring you can face whatever the future holds with confidence and grace.

Why Planning Matters

Throughout this book, we've explored the importance of planning for your financial, legal, and personal needs. A thoughtful plan is your safety net, ensuring your wishes will be respected even if you can no longer advocate for yourself. Without a plan, you risk leaving crucial decisions to strangers or the court system—people who may not know or prioritize what truly matters to you.

Planning involves more than documents; it's about creating a roadmap for your life that aligns with your values and priorities. It's about taking control of your story.

The Power of People

No plan is complete without people. Solo seniors often face unique challenges in identifying and trusting individuals to step into key roles like Health Care Proxy, Power of Attorney, or even just a supportive friend in times of need. Building and nurturing a network of reliable people is a cornerstone of thriving.

These people can be friends, neighbors, professionals, or fellow solo seniors who share your journey. As we've seen in examples throughout this book, creativity and connection can turn the challenge of aging alone into an opportunity to forge meaningful relationships.

Inspiration from Real Life

I have been inspired by the creative and proactive approaches solo seniors have taken. From the solo senior network in Winchester to the group of women who formed their own mutual support system, these examples show what's possible when people take the initiative to plan and connect.

If this idea resonates with you—if you're interested in leading or being part of a local group of solo seniors—I invite you to visit www.soloallies.com and complete a short form. If there's enough interest in your area, I will do my best to connect you with others who share the same goal. Together, we can build something meaningful—connections that bring both social and practical support.

The Road Ahead

As you close this book, I encourage you to take the first step toward your future. Review the planning tools and resources provided in these pages. Consider your personal goals, and identify the people who can support you. Then, take action. Start small, but start today.

A Final Thought

Thriving as a solo senior is not about perfection—it's about empowerment. Planning ahead and building relationships create a foundation for peace of mind. By doing so, you ensure that your future reflects your values, priorities, and wishes.

Thank you for reading this book. My hope is that it has given you the tools, inspiration, and confidence to take control of your future—and truly thrive.

> *"May the road rise to meet you. May the wind be always at your back. May the sun shine warm upon your face; the rains fall soft upon your fields, and until we meet again, may God hold you in the palm of his hand."*
>
> *- An Irish Blessing*

SOLOALLIES.COM
YOUR RESOURCE FOR PLANNING, CONNECTION, AND SUPPORT

Aging alone comes with unique challenges, but Solo Allies is here to help. I created www.soloallies.com as an online resource specifically designed for those planning for their future without immediate family support. Whether you are looking for practical tools, professional guidance, or a supportive community, Solo Allies offers valuable solutions.

What You Will Find on SoloAllies.Com

- **Planning Tools & Worksheets** – Organize important information with easy-to-use free templates, including an In Case of Emergency form and the Solo Senior Organizer.

- **DIY Estate Planning Documents** – Complete a questionnaire to create custom estate planning documents for solo seniors (currently available for Massachusetts, with plans to expand to other states).

- **Directory of Professionals** – Find elder law attorneys and other professionals to support you.

- **Opportunities to Connect** – We plan to launch initiatives to help you connect with other solo seniors. Express your interest in joining an online coaching, community forum, or local regional group.

Join Us & Take the Next Step

If you are looking for practical guidance and a way to build a supportive network, I invite you to visit www.soloallies.com. Explore the tools, sign up for updates, and discover how planning and connection can give you peace of mind.

You are not alone in this journey.
Let's build a future where solo seniors can thrive together!

Kathy McNair is an Elder Law attorney who has spent more than 25 years helping seniors plan for the future with dignity and peace of mind. Her passion for this work began early in her career, when judges appointed her as Guardian and Conservator for seniors who had no one else.

She would often meet these clients for the first time in a hospital room, in the midst of a health or mental health crisis. It was a painful moment for everyone. Kathy was a stranger, now charged with making life-altering decisions about their care, money, and future. She never had the chance to know them before they declined—or to understand what mattered most to them.

That experience shaped everything she does today.

Kathy now focuses on helping seniors, especially those aging alone, plan ahead before a crisis happens.

In 2001, Kathy founded Senior Solutions LLC, Attorneys at Law, where she provides services in Medicaid Planning, Estate Planning, Probate, and Special Needs Trusts. For fifteen years, she served a Public Administrator of Suffolk County, managing estates for those who died without known heirs. She currently serves on the Board of Directors for McNamara House, an affordable senior housing community in Boston.

Kathy earned her law degree from Boston College Law School and her undergraduate degree in Psychology from St. Lawrence University.

She lives in Boston and enjoys spending time with her family, being outdoors and active, and improving her pickleball skills.

PART IV:
SOLO SENIOR ORGANIZER

*"It takes as much energy
to wish as it does to plan."*

—*Eleanor Roosevelt*

ORGANIZING YOUR EMERGENCY CONTACTS AND IMPORTANT INFORMATION

This part of the book, The Solo Senior Organizer, is designed to help you organize vital information that will be needed in case of an emergency, incapacity, or after your passing.

By completing these pages, you can ensure that your trusted individuals or professionals have the information they need to act quickly and effectively on your behalf.

However, I want to emphasize that:

This organizer is not a substitute for legal planning documents. At a minimum you should have:

- *A Health Care Proxy*
- *A Power of Attorney*
- *A Last Will and Testament.*

You are NOT creating the above legal documents by filling out these pages.

If you need assistance creating legal documents designed for the unique circumstances of solo seniors, please visit Solo Allies (http://www.soloallies.com) for resources and a directory of attorneys in your area who may be able to assist you.

There are two ways to complete the following pages:

- Fill in your information in this book and then cut out the pages.
- Download and print the organizer as a PDF from https://www.soloallies.com/worksheetdownload for free.

HOW TO USE
THE SOLO SENIOR ORGANIZER

- If you are using the pages included here, cut them out to separate them from the book. This way, they will be easier to store and locate among your other estate planning documents.

- Alternatively, you can download the Solo Senior Organizer as a PDF, print it out, and fill it in by hand. https://www.soloallies.com/worksheetdownload

- Complete all sections of the Solo Senior Organizer to the best of your ability.

- Store your Solo Senior Organizer in a secure but accessible location, along with your estate planning documents.

- Make a copy of the completed Emergency Contact Information sheets to display in a prominent place in your home, for example, on your refrigerator.

- Give copies of your Solo Senior Organizer to the people that you trust to be there for you in an emergency or let them know how they can find it when it is needed.

- Update the information in your Solo Senior Organizer periodically to keep the information current.

MY BASIC INFORMATION

Full Legal Name: _____

_____

Other Names: _____

_____

Date of Birth: _____

_____

Home Address: _____

_____

_____

_____

Cell Phone: _____

Other Phones: _____

Email: _____

Notes: _____

_____

_____

EMERGENCY CONTACTS

In case of a health emergency, please contact my

Health Care Proxy

Name:

Relationship To Me:

Cell Phone:

Other Phones:

Email:

Address:

Notes:

EMERGENCY CONTACTS

If my Health Care Proxy cannot be contacted, please contact my
Back-Up Health Care Proxy

Name:

Relationship To Me:

Cell Phone:

Other Phones:

Email:

Address:

Notes:

EMERGENCY CONTACTS

If case of a health emergency, please contact my

Primary Care Doctor

Name: _____

_____

Office Address: _____

_____

_____

_____

Office Phone: _____

Other Phones: _____

_____

Email: _____

Notes: _____

_____

_____

_____

OTHER IMPORTANT CONTACTS

(Attorney, Neighbor, Friend, Pastor, Pet Sitter,
Financial Advisor, Accountant, etc.)

Name:

Cell Phone:

Other Phones:

Email:

Address:

Relationship To Me:

Reason for Contacting:

OTHER IMPORTANT CONTACTS

(Attorney, Neighbor, Friend, Pastor, Pet Sitter,
Financial Advisor, Accountant, etc.)

Name:

Cell Phone:

Other Phones:

Email:

Address:

Relationship To Me:

Reason for Contacting:

OTHER IMPORTANT CONTACTS

(Attorney, Neighbor, Friend, Pastor, Pet Sitter,
Financial Advisor, Accountant, etc.)

Name:

Cell Phone:

Other Phones:

Email:

Address:

Relationship To Me:

Reason for Contacting:

EMERGENCY INSTRUCTIONS

Do you have any allergies, key medical conditions, or critical medication that first responders should be aware of? Are there any hospitals you prefer or wish to avoid?

PREFERENCES FOR CARE

If your health or cognitive abilities decline, where would you like to live?

- At home with private assistance.

- In an assisted living or Memory Care facility. Do you have a preference?

- If a nursing home becomes the only option, do you have a preference?

In addition to your Health Care Proxy, do you have an Advanced Directive? (If so, keep a copy with this document. If not, describe how you feel about end-of-life care, in your own words here.)

HEALTH INSURANCE

Provider (Medicare, Blue Cross, etc.): _____

_____

_____

_____

Policy No: _____

_____

_____

Coverage Type (General Health, Dental, Vision, MedEx Supplement, etc.):

_____

_____

_____

_____

Additional Health Insurance Notes: _____

_____

_____

_____

ESTATE PLANNING CONTACTS

I have chose the following person to act as my
Power of Attorney (Primary)

Name:

Cell Phone:

Other Phones:

Email:

Address:

Notes:

ESTATE PLANNING CONTACTS

If my Primary Power of Attorney cannot serve, please contact
Power of Attorney (Successor)

Name:

Cell Phone:

Other Phones:

Email:

Address:

Notes:

ESTATE PLANNING CONTACTS

I have appointed this person to manage my estate after I die:

Executor (Personal Representative)

Name:

Cell Phone:

Other Phones:

Email:

Address:

Notes:

ESTATE PLANNING CONTACTS

If my Executor (Personal Representative) cannot serve, contact

Executor (Successor)

Name:

Cell Phone:

Other Phones:

Email:

Address:

Notes:

COMPLETING YOUR FINANCIAL AND TANGIBLE ASSET INFORMATION

In this section, please provide information about your financial assets, such as real estate, businesses, bank accounts, investments, retirements accounts, annuities, insurance, and more. If you need more space, you can add a spreadsheet or other pages.

In addition to basic information about each asset, such as property addresses, account numbers, and financial institutions, please fill in the following:

Co-owner(s) – If you jointly own an asset with other people, give their names.

Title – "Title" refers to the name(s) listed on the account or asset. Financial accounts, real estate or trusts can be titled in several ways, for example:

- In an individual's name alone (e.g., "Joan Doe")
- Jointly with another person (e.g., "Joan Doe and John Doe")
- In the name of a trust (e.g., "The Joan Doe Revocable Trust")

Estimated Value – Provide the dollar amount of the asset's value at the time when you complete the Organizer.

FINANCIAL ACCOUNTS
(Bank Accounts, CDs)

Bank Name: _____

_____

Account Type: _____

Account No: _____

Co-Owner(s) on Title: _____

_____

Estimated Value: _____

Bank Name: _____

_____

Account Type: _____

Account No: _____

Co-Owner(s) on Title: _____

_____

Estimated Value: _____

FINANCIAL ACCOUNTS
(Bank Accounts, CDs)

Bank Name: _____

_____

Account Type: _____

Account No: _____

Co-Owner(s) on Title: _____

_____

Estimated Value: _____

Bank Name: _____

_____

Account Type: _____

Account No: _____

Co-Owner(s) on Title: _____

_____

Estimated Value: _____

RETIREMENT ACCOUNTS
(401K, IRA, Pension, etc.)

Bank/Brokerage Name: _____

_____

_____

Account Type: _____

Account No: _____

Employer Plan (Yes/No): _____

Estimated Value: _____

Bank/Brokerage Name: _____

_____

_____

Account Type: _____

Account No: _____

Employer Plan (Yes/No): _____

Estimated Value: _____

INVESTMENT ACCOUNTS
(Brokerage, Stocks, Bonds, Mutual Funds, etc.)

Bank/Brokerage Name: _____

_____

_____

Account Type: _____

Account No: _____

Co-Owner(s): _____

Estimated Value: _____

Bank/Brokerage Name: _____

_____

_____

Account Type: _____

Account No: _____

Co-Owner (s): _____

Estimated Value: _____

ANNUITIES
(Investment-Based or Insurance-Based)

Provider: _____

_____

Policy/Account No: _____

Type (Fixed, Variable, Indexed, etc.): _____

_____

Beneficiaries: _____

Monthly/Annual Payout: _____

Provider: _____

_____

Policy/Account No: _____

Type (Fixed, Variable, Indexed, etc.): _____

_____

Beneficiaries: _____

Monthly/Annual Payout: _____

LIFE INSURANCE

Insurance Company:

Policy No:

Type (Term Life, Whole Life, Universal Life, Group, etc.):

Coverage Amount ($):

Beneficiary Name(s):

Start Date:

Notes:

REAL ESTATE

Property Address:

_____

_____

_____

Co-owner(s): _____

Name(s) Listed on Title: _____

_____

Estimated Value: _____

Property Address:

_____

_____

_____

Co-owner(s): _____

Name(s) Listed on Title: _____

_____

Estimated Value: _____

BUSINESS ASSETS
(Partnership / LLC / S-Corp, etc.)

Business Name:

Type (LLC,S-Corp, etc):

Address/URL:

Co-owner(s):

Estimated Value:

Notes:

TANGIBLE PROPERTY

Vehicles, Art, Jewelry, Antiques, Collectibles, Precious Metals, etc. Please provide a description of each item, its estimated value, and its location.

OTHER HIGH-VALUE PROPERTY

High-value items (financial or sentimental) that need to be transferred or sold (e.g., cryptocurrency, musical instruments, firearms, cemetery plots, time shares, storage units).

LIABILITIES

Do you have any outstanding mortgages, loans, credit card balances, business debts, taxes, etc.? Please list them here.

OTHER IMPORTANT INFORMATION

In the following pages, please provide information about items you have in safekeeping—what they are, where they are stored, and how they can be accessed.

Please answer the provided questions to remind your Health Care Proxy and Power of Attorney about your wishes. For things not covered in the questions, you can make notes on the last page and attach additional pages as needed.

ITEMS IN SAFEKEEPING

Cash, Bonds, Bearer Certificates, Keys & Access Tools, Flashdrives, etc.

OTHER KEY INFORMATION

Does anyone owe you money? (Person, amount, reason)

_____

_____

_____

_____

Do you have safe deposit box at a bank? (Note: You must add someone as a signer to access this account.)

_____

_____

_____

Do you keep large amounts of cash or valuable belongings ($10,000+) at home? List them here:

_____

_____

_____

_____

_____

OTHER KEY INFORMATION

Does anyone have a key to your home that can be used in an emergency?

_____

_____

Where are your estate planning documents kept? Who has the original documents?

_____

_____

If you have a pet, please provide information such as type of pet, name, age, and veterinarian:

_____

_____

_____

_____

_____

_____

FUNERAL/BURIAL INFORMATION

Do you have any specific instructions for your funeral arrangements? If so, please provide this information here:

_____

_____

_____

_____

Have you prepaid any funeral or burial arrangements? If so, please provide information here.

_____

_____

_____

_____

_____

_____

_____

_____

_____

_____

OTHER KEY INFORMATION

Please provide any additional information you want your Health Care Proxy and Power of Attorney to know.

STORING, SHARING, AND UPDATING YOUR SOLO SENIOR ORGANIZER

Keep your Solo Senior Organizer with your estate planning documents. Let your Power of Attorney know where they can find this planner or if you feel comfortable and trust this person, give them a copy now. It will help them be prepared if they need it.

If you have a Health Care Proxy document, give it to your primary care doctor and ask that it be included in your medical record.

Be careful about sharing your personal information with others, and please avoid scams.

Please review the information in the Solo Senior Organizer annually or whenever there is a significant change in your circumstances. By completing these pages, having valid legal documents in place, and making sure that you have people to count on, you should be in good shape. I hope this brings you peace of mind.

• • • •

If you need further guidance or you are overwhelmed about planning for your future, www.soloallies.com offers resources and planning tools (including DIY planning tools) and partners with attorneys, such as Senior Solutions Attorneys at Law (www.seniorsolutionsinfo.com) to provide one-on-one estate planning services.

Thank you for reading!

*If you found The Solo Senior's Guide to Thrive
helpful and believe it might help someone else,
I would be grateful if you would leave a review
on Amazon.*

Your feedback helps others discover the book.

*Thank you for your support.
Kathy McNair*

www.ingramcontent.com/pod-product-compliance
Lightning Source LLC
Chambersburg PA
CBHW071603210326
41597CB00019B/3388